THE COMIC LATIN GRAMMAR

LECTOR HOUSE PUBLIC DOMAIN WORKS

HAPPY READING!

THE COMIC LATIN GRAMMAR

PERCIVAL LEIGH

ISBN: 978-93-5614-140-7

Published: 1840

© 2022
LECTOR HOUSE LLP

LECTOR HOUSE

LECTOR HOUSE LLP
E-MAIL: lectorpublishing@gmail.com

Drawn and Engraved by John Leech. R.C.A.

THE COMIC LATIN GRAMMAR;

A NEW AND FACETIOUS INTRODUCTION TO THE LATIN TONGUE.

BY

PERCIVAL LEIGH

WITH NUMEROUS ILLUSTRATIONS.

THE SECOND EDITION.

MDCCCXL.

ADVERTISEMENT
TO THE SECOND EDITION.

The Author of this little work cannot allow a second edition of it to go forth to the world, unaccompanied by a few words of apology, he being desirous of imitating, in every respect, the example of distinguished writers.

He begs that so much as the consciousness of being answerable for a great deal of nonsense, usually prompts a man to say, in the hope of disarming criticism, may be considered to have been said already. But he particularly requests that the want of additions to his book may be excused; and pleads, in arrest of judgment, his numerous and absorbing avocations.

Wishing to atone as much as possible for this deficiency, and prevailed upon by the importunity of his friends, he has allowed a portrait of himself, by that eminent artist, Mr. John Leech, to whom he is indebted for the embellishments, and very probably for the sale of the book, to be presented, facing the title-page, to the public.

Here again he has been influenced by the wish to comply with the requisitions of custom, and the disinclination to appear odd, whimsical, or peculiar.

On the admirable sketch itself, bare justice requires that he should speak somewhat in detail. The likeness he is told, he fears by too partial admirers, is excellent. The principle on which it has been executed, that of investing with an ideal magnitude, the proportions of nature, is plainly, from what we observe in heroic poetry, painting, and sculpture, the soul itself of the superhuman and sublime. Of the justness of the metaphorical compliment implied in the delineation of the head, it is not for the author to speak; of its exquisiteness and delicacy, his sense is too strong for expression. The habitual pensiveness of the elevated eyebrows, mingled with the momentary gaiety of the rest of the countenance, is one of the most successful points in the picture, and is as true to nature as it is indicative of art.

The Author's tailor, though there are certain reasons why his name should not appear in print, desires to express his obligation to the talented artist for the very favourable impression which, without prejudice to truth, has been given to the public of his skill. The ease so conspicuous in the management of the surtout, and the thought so remarkable in the treatment of the trousers, fully warrant his admiration and gratitude.

Too great praise cannot be bestowed on the boots, considered with reference to art, though in this respect the Author is quite sensible that both himself and the maker of their originals have been greatly flattered. He is also perfectly aware that there is a degree of neatness, elegance, and spirit in the tie of the cravat, to which he has in reality never yet been able to attain.

In conclusion, he is much gratified by the taste displayed in furnishing him with so handsome a walking stick; and he assures all whom it may concern, that the hint thus bestowed will not be lost upon him; for he intends immediately to relinquish the large oaken cudgel which he has hitherto been accustomed to carry, and to appear, in every respect, to the present generation, such as he will descend to posterity.

PREFACE.

A GREAT book, says an old proverb, is a great evil; and a great preface, says a new one, is a great bore. It is not, therefore, our intention to expatiate largely on the present occasion; especially since a long discourse prefixed to a small volume, is like a forty-eight pounder at the door of a pig-stye. We should as soon think of erecting the Nelson Memorial in front of Buckingham Palace. Indeed, were it not necessary to show some kind of respect to fashion, we should hasten at once into the midst of things, instead of trespassing on the patience of our readers, and possibly, trifling with their time. We should not like to be kept waiting at a Lord Mayor's feast by a long description of the bill of fare. Our preface, however, shall at least have the merit of novelty; it shall be candid.

This book, like the razors in Dr. Wolcot's story, is made to *sell*. This last word has a rather equivocal meaning—but we scorn to blot, otherwise we should say to be sold. An article offered for sale may, nevertheless, be worth buying; and it is hoped that the resemblance between the aforesaid razors, and this our production, does not extend to the respective *sharpness* of the commodities. The razors proved scarcely worth a farthing to the clown who bought them for eighteen-pence, and were fit to shave nothing but the beard of an oyster. We trust that the "Comic Latin Grammar" will be found to *cut*, now and then, rather better, at least, than that comes to; and that it will reward the purchaser, at any rate, with his pennyworth for his penny, by its genuine bonâ fide contents. There are many works, the pages of which contain a good deal of useful matter—sometimes in the shape of an ounce of tea or a pound of butter: we venture to indulge the expectation, that these latter additions to the value of our own, will be considered unnecessary.

Perhaps we should have adopted the title of "Latin in sport made learning in earnest"—which would give a tolerable idea of the nature of our undertaking. The doctrine, it is true, may bear the same relation to the lighter matter, that the bread in Falstaff's private account did to the liquor; though if we have given our reader "a deal of sack," we wish it may not be altogether "intolerable." Latin, however, is a great deal less like bread, to most boys, than it is like physic; especially *antimony*, *ipecacuanha*, and similar medicines. It ought, therefore, to be given in something palatable, and capable of causing it to be retained by the—mind—in what physicians call a pleasant vehicle. This we have endeavoured to invent—and if we have disguised the flavour of the drugs without destroying their virtues, we shall have entirely accomplished our design. There are a few particularly nasty pills, draughts, and boluses, which we could find no means of sweetening; and with which, on that account, we have not attempted to meddle. For these omissions we must request some little indulgence. Our performance is confessedly imperfect, but be it remembered, that

> "Men rather do their broken weapons use,
> Than their bare hands."

The "Comic Latin Grammar" can, certainly, never be called an *imposition*, as another Latin Grammar frequently is. We remember having had the whole of it to learn at school, besides being—no matter what—for pinning a cracker to the master's coat-tail. The above hint is worthy the attention of boys; nor will the following, probably, be thrown away upon school-masters, particularly such as reside in the north of England. "Laugh and grow fat," is an ancient and a true maxim. Now, will not the "Comic Latin Grammar," (like Scotch marmalade and Yarmouth bloaters) form a "desirable addition" to the breakfast of the young gentlemen entrusted to their care? We dare not say much of its superseding the use of the cane, as we hold all old established customs in the utmost reverence and respect; and, besides, have no wish to deprive any one of innocent amusement. We would only suggest, that flagellation is now *sometimes* necessary, and that whatever tends to render it *optional* may, now and then, save trouble.

One word in conclusion. The march of intellect is not confined to the male sex; the fairer part of the creation are now augmenting by their numbers, and adorning by their countenance, the scientific and literary train. But the path of learning is sometimes too rugged for their tender feet. We pretend not to strew it for them with roses; we are not poetically given—nay, we cannot even promise them a Brussels carpet;—but if a plain Kidderminster will serve their turn, we here display one for their accommodation, that thus smoothly and pleasantly they may make their safe ascent to the temple of Minerva and the Muses.

CONTENTS

LIST OF ETCHINGS

INTRODUCTION.

Very little introductory matter would probably be sufficient to place the rising generation on terms of the most perfect familiarity with a "Comic Latin Grammar." To the elder and middle-aged portion of the community, however, the very notion of such a work may seem in the highest degree preposterous; if not indicative of a degree of presumptuous irreverence on the part of the author little short of literary high treason, if not commensurate, in point of moral delinquency, with the same crime as defined by the common law of England. It is out of consideration for the praiseworthy, though perhaps erroneous, feelings of such respectable personages, that we proceed to make the following preliminary remarks; wherein it will be our object, by demonstrating the necessity which exists for such a publication as the present, to exonerate ourselves from all blame on the score of its production.

When we consider the progress of civilization and refinement, we find that all ages have in turn been characterized by some one distinctive peculiarity or other. To say nothing of the Golden Age, the Silver Age, the Iron Age, and so forth, which, with all possible respect for the poets, can scarcely be said to be worth much in a grave argument; it is quite clear that the Augustan Age, the Middle Ages, the Elizabethan Age, and the Age of Queen Anne, were all of them very different, one from the other, in regard to the peculiar tone of feeling which distinguished the public mind in each of them. In like manner, the present (which will hereafter probably be called the Victorian Age) is very unlike all that have preceded it. It may be termed the Age of Comicality. Not but that some traces of comic feeling, inherent as it is in the very nature of man, have not at all times been more or less observable; but it is only of late years that the ludicrous capabilities of the human mind have expanded in their fullest vigour. Comicality has heretofore been evinced only, as it were, in isolated sparks and flashes, instead of that full blaze of meridian splendour which now pervades the entire mechanism of society, and illuminates all the transactions of life. Thus in the Golden Age, there was something very comical in human creatures eating acorns, like pigs. The Augustan Age was comical enough, if we may trust some of Horace's satires. Much comicality was displayed in the Middle Ages, in the proceedings of the knights errant, the doings in Palestine, and the mode adopted by the priests of inculcating religion on the minds of the people. In the Elizabethan Age several comic incidents occurred at court; particularly when any of the courtiers were guilty of personal impertinence to their virgin queen. It must have been very comical to see Shakspere holding stirrups like an ostler, or performing the part of the Ghost, in his own play of Hamlet. The dress worn in Queen Anne's time, and that of the first Georges, was very comical indeed—but enough of this. Our concern is with the present time—the funniest epoch, beyond all comparison, in the history of the world. Some few years back, the minds of nations, convulsed with the great political revolutions then taking place, were in a mood by no means apt to be gratified by whimsicality and merriment. Furthermore, certain poets of the lack-a-daisical school, such as Byron, Shelley, Goethe, and others, writing in conformity with the prevailing taste of the day, threw a wet blanket on the spirits of men, which all but extinguished the feeble embers of mirth, upon which 'shocking events' had exercised so pernicious an influence already: or, to change a vulgar for a scientific metaphor, they placed such a pressure of sentimental atmosphere on the common stock of laughing gas, as to convert it into a mere fluid, and almost to solidify it altogether. It is now exhibiting the amazing amount of expansive force, which under favourable circumstances it is capable of exerting. Many causes have combined to bring about the happy state of things under which we now live. Amongst these, the exertions of individuals hold the first rank; of whom the veteran Liston, the late lamented Mr. John Reeve, the facetious Keeley, and the inimitable Buckstone, are deserving of our highest commendation. And more especially is praise due to the talented author of the Pickwick Papers, whose genius has convulsed the sides of thousands, has revolutionized the republic of letters (making, no doubt, a great many *sovereigns*) and has become, as it were, a mirror, which will reflect to all posterity the laughter-loving spirit of his age.

But it is not (as we have before remarked) in literature alone, that the tendency to the ludicrous is shewn. In many recent scientific speculations it is strikingly and abundantly obvious—some of those on geology may be quoted as examples. The offspring of the sciences—those pledges of affection which they present to art, almost all of them, come into the world with a caricature-like smirk upon their faces. Air-balloons and rail-roads have something funny about them; and photogenic drawings are, to say the least, very curious. The learned professions are all tinged with drollery. The law is confessedly ridiculous from beginning to end, and what is very strange, is that no one should attempt to make it otherwise. Medicine is comical—or rather tragi-comical—the disparity of opinion among its professors, the chaotic state of its principles, and the conduct of its students being considered. No one can deny that the distribution of church property is somewhat *odd*, or can assert that the doings—at least of those who are destined for the clerical office, are now and then of rather a strange character. Political meetings are very laughable things, when we reflect upon the strong asseverations of patriotism there made and believed. The wisdom of the legislature is by no means of the gravest class, particularly when it offers municipal reforms as a substitute for bread. The debates in a certain House must be of a very humourous character, if we may judge from the frequent "hear hear, and a laugh," by which the proceedings there are interrupted. Our risible faculties are continually called into action at public lectures of all kinds; and indeed, no lecturer, however learned he may be, has much chance now-a-days of instructing, unless he can also amuse his audience. Nor can the various public and even private buildings, which are daily springing up around us, like so many mushrooms, be contemplated without considerable emotions of mirthfulness. The new style of ecclesiastical architecture, entitled the Cockney-Gothic, affords a good illustration of this remark; but the comic Temple of the Fine Arts, in Trafalgar Square, is what Lord Bacon would have called a "glaring instance" of its correctness. The occurrences of the day bear all of them the stamp of facetiousness. The vote of approbation, lately passed on a certain course of policy, is a capital joke; the tricks that are constantly played off upon John Bull by the Russians, French, Yankees, and others, though somewhat impertinent to the aforesaid John, must seem very diverting to lookers on. The state of the Drama may also be brought forward in proof of our position. Tragedies are at a discount; farces are at a premium; lions, nay goats and monkeys, are pressed into the service of Momus. Even the various institutions for the advancement of morals have not escaped the influence of the prevailing taste. To mention that respectable body of men, the Teetotallers, is sufficient of itself to excite a smile. In short, look wherever you will, you will find it a matter of the greatest difficulty to keep your countenance.

The truth is, that people are tired of crying, and find it much more agreeable to laugh. The sublime is out of fashion; the ridiculous is in vogue. A turn-up nose is now a more interesting object than a turn-down collar; and if it should be urged that the flowing locks of our young men are indicative of sentimentality by their *length*, let it be remembered that they are in general quite unaccompanied by a corresponding quality of face. It has been said that the schoolmaster is abroad:—true; but he is walking arm and arm with the Merry-Andrew; and the members, presidents, and secretaries of mechanics' institutions, and associations for the advancement of everything, follow in his train. Nothing can be taught that is not palatable, and nothing is now palatable but what is funny. That boys should be instructed in the Latin language will be denied by few (although by some eccentric persons this has been done); that they can be expected to learn what they cannot laugh at will, to all reflecting minds, especially on perusing the foregoing considerations, appear in the highest degree unreasonable. To conclude:—let all such as are disposed to stare at the title of our work, ponder attentively on what we have said above; let them, in the language of the farce, "put this and that together," and they will at once perceive the beneficial effect, which holding up the Latin Grammar to ridicule is likely to produce in the minds of youth. So much for the satisfaction of our senior readers. And now, no longer to detain our juvenile friends, let us proceed to business, or pleasure, or both:—we will not stand upon ceremony with respect to terms.

THE SCHOOLMASTER ABROAD.

THE COMIC LATIN GRAMMAR.

Of Latin there are three kinds: Latin Proper, or good Latin; Dog Latin; and Thieves' Latin, Latin Proper, or good Latin, is the language which was spoken by the ancient Romans. Dog Latin is the Latin in which boys compose their first verses and themes, and which is occasionally employed at the Universities of Oxford and Cambridge, but much more frequently at Edinburgh, Aberdeen, and Glasgow. It includes Medical Latin, and Law Latin; though these, to the unlearned, generally appear Greek. Mens tuus ego—mind your eye; Illic vadis cum oculo tuo ex—there you go with your eye out; Quomodo est mater tua?—how's your mother? Fiat haustus ter die capiendus—let a draught be made, to be taken three times a day; Bona et catalla—goods and chattels—are examples.

A HEAVY SWELL.

Thieves' Latin, more commonly known by the name of slang, is much in use among a certain class of *conveyancers,* who disregard the distinctions of meum and tuum. Furthermore, it constitutes a great part of the familiar discourse of most young men in modern times, particularly lawyers' clerks and medical students.

It bears a very close affinity to Law Latin, with which, indeed, it is sometimes confounded. Examples:—to prig a wipe—to steal a handkerchief. A rum start—a curious occurrence. A plant—an imposition. Flummoxed—undone. Sold—deceived. A heavy swell—a great dandy. Quibus, tin, dibs, mopuses, stumpy—money. Grub, prog, tuck—victuals. A stiff-'un—a dead body—properly, a subject. To be scragged—to suffer the last penalty of the law, &c.

All these kinds of Latin are to be taught in the Comic Latin Grammar.

*   *   *   *   *

TOBY, THE LEARNED PIG.

If Toby, the learned pig, had been desired to say his alphabet in Latin, he would have done it by taking away the W from the English alphabet. Indeed, this is what he is said to have actually done. The Latin letters, therefore, remind us of the greatest age that a fashionable lady ever confesses she has attained to,—being between twenty and thirty.

Six of these letters are called what Dutchmen, speaking English, call fowls—vowels; namely, a, e, i, o, u, y.

A vowel is like an Æolian harp; it makes a full and perfect sound of itself. A consonant cannot sound without a vowel, any more than a horn (except such an one as Baron Munchausen's) can play a tune without a performer.

Consonants are divided into mutes, liquids and double letters; although they have nothing in particular to do with funerals, hydrostatics, or the General post office. The liquids are, l, m, n, r; the double letters, j, x, z; the other letters are mutes.

"Hye dum, dye dum, fiddle *dumb*—c." —STERNE.

A syllable is a distinct sound of one or more letters pronounced in a breath, or, as we say in the classics, in a jiffey.

A HUMAN DIPHTHONG.

A diphthong is the sound of two vowels in one syllable. Taken collectively they resemble a closed fist—i.e. a bunch of *fives*. The diphthongs are au, eu, ei, æ, and œ. Of the two first of these, au and eu, the sound is *intermediate* between that of the two vowels of which each is formed. This fact may perhaps be impressed upon the mind, on the principles of artificial memory, by a reference to a familiar beverage, known by the name of half-and-half. In like manner, ei, which is generally pronounced i, and æ and œ, sounded like e, may be said to exhibit something like an analogy to a married couple. The human diphthong, Smith female + Brown male, is called Brown only.

The reason, says the fool in King Lear, why the seven stars are no more than seven—is a pretty reason—because they are not eight. This is a fool's reason; but we (like many other commentators) cannot give a better one, why the Parts of Speech are no more than eight—because they are not nine. They are as follow:

1. Noun, Pronoun, Verb, Participle—declined.

2. Adverb, Preposition, Conjunction, Interjection—undeclined. Most school-boys would like to decline them altogether.

*   *   *   *   *

OF A NOUN.

A noun is a name,—whether it be a Christian name, or a sur-name—the name of a prince, a pig, a pancake, or a post. Whatever is—is a noun.

Nouns are divided into substantives and adjectives.

A noun substantive is its own trumpeter, and speaks for itself without assistance from any other word—brassica, a cabbage; sartor, a tailor; medicus, a physician; vetula, an old woman; venenum, poison; are examples of substantives.

MACER PUER.

PINGUIS PUER.

An adjective is like an infant in leading strings—it cannot go alone. It always requires to be joined to a substantive, of which it shows the nature or quality—as lectio longa, a long lesson; magnus aper, a great *boar*; pinguis puer, a fat boy; macer puer, a lean boy. In making love (as you will find one of these days) or in abusing a cab-man, your success will depend in no small degree in your choice of adjectives.

*   *   *   *   *

NUMBERS OF NOUNS.

Be not alarmed, boys, at the above heading. There are numbers of nouns, it is true, that is to say, lots; or, as we say in the schools, "a precious sight" of nouns in the dictionary; but we are not now going to enumerate, and make you learn them. The numbers of nouns here spoken of are two only; the singular and the plural.

The singular speaks but of one—as later, a brick; faba, a bean; tuba, a trump (or trumpet); flamma, a blaze; æthiops, a nigger (or negro); cornix, a crow.

The plural speaks of more than one—as lateres, bricks; fabæ, beans; tubæ, trumps; flammæ, blazes; æthiopes, niggers; cornices, crows.

Here it may be remarked that the cynic philosophers were very *singular* fellows.

Also that prize-poems are sometimes composed in very *singular numbers*.

*   *   *   *   *

A DATIVE AND A VOCATIVE CASE
(SCHOOLMASTER SPATTING A BOY).

CASES OF NOUNS.

Nouns have six cases in each number, (that is, six of one and half a dozen of the other) but can only be put in one of them at a time. They are thus ticketed — nominative, genitive, dative, accusative, vocative, and ablative.

The nominative case comes before the verb, as the horse does before the cart, the "lieutenant before the ancient," and the superintendant of police before the inspector. It answers to the question, who or what; as, Who jaws? *magister jurgatur*, the master jaws.

The genitive case is known by the sign of, and answers to the question, whose, or whereof; as, Whose breeches? *Femoralia magistri* — the breeches of the master, or the master's breeches.

The dative case is known by the signs to or for, and answers to the question, to whom, or to or for what; as, To whom do I hold out my hands? *Protendo manus magistro* — I hold out my hands to the master.

In this place we are called upon to consider, whether it be more agreeable to have Latin or the ferula at our *fingers' ends*.

Observe that *dative* means *giving*. Schoolmasters are very often in the dative case — but their generosity is chiefly exercised in bestowing what is termed monkey's allowance; that is, if not more kicks, more boxes on the ear, more spats, more canings, birchings, and impositions, than halfpence.

The accusative case follows the verb, as a bailiff follows a debtor, a bull-dog a butcher, or a round of applause a supernatural squall at the Italian Opera. It answers to the question Whom? or What? as, Whom do you laugh at? (behind his back) *Derideo magistrum* — I laugh at the master.

The vocative case is known by calling, or speaking to; as, O magister — O master; an exclamation which is frequently the consequence of shirking out, making false concords or quantities, obstreperous conduct in school, &c.

The ablative case is known by certain prepositions, expressed or understood; as Deprensus magistro — caught out by the master. Coram *rostro* — before the *beak*. The prepositions, in, with, from, by, and the word, than, after the comparative degree, are signs of the ablative case. In angustiâ — in a fix. Cum indigenâ — with a native. Ab arbore — from a tree. A rictu — by a grin. Adipe lubricior — slicker than grease.

*   *   *   *   *

GENDERS AND ARTICLES.

The genders of nouns, which are three, the masculine, the feminine, and the neuter, are denoted in Latin by articles. We have articles, also, in English, which distinguish the masculine from the feminine, but they are articles of dress; such as petticoats and breeches, mantillas and mackintoshes. But as there are many things in Latin, called masculine and feminine, which are nevertheless not male and female, the articles attached to them are not parts of dress, but parts of speech.

MASC.   **FEM.**

We will now, with our readers' permission, initiate them into a new mode of declining the article hic, hæc, hoc. And we take this opportunity of protesting against the old and short-sighted system of teaching a boy only one thing at a time, which originated, no doubt, from the general ignorance of everything but the dead languages which prevailed in the monkish ages. We propose to make declensions, conjugations, &c., a vehicle for imparting something more than the mere dry facts of the immediate subject. And if we can occasionally inculcate an original remark, a scientific principle, or a moral aphorism, we shall, of course, think ourselves sufficiently rewarded by the consciousness—et cætera, et cætera, et cætera.

Masc. hic.   Fem. hæc.   Neut. hoc, &c.

The nominative singular's hic, hæc, and hoc,—
Which to learn, has cost school boys full many a knock;
The genitive 's hujus, the dative makes huic,
(A fact Mr. Squeers never mentioned to Smike);
Then hunc, hanc, and hoc, the accusative makes,
The vocative—caret—no very great shakes;
The ablative case maketh hôc, hac, and hôc,
A cock is a fowl—but a fowl 's not a cock.
The nominative plural is hi, hæ, and hæc,
The Roman young ladies were dressed à la Grecque;

The genitive case horum, harum, and horum,
Silenus and Bacchus were fond of a jorum;
The dative in all the three genders is his,
At Actium his tip did Mark Antony miss:
The accusative 's hos, has, and hæc in all grammars,
Herodotus told some American crammers;
The vocative here also—caret— 's no go,
As Milo found rending an oak-tree, you know;
And his, like the dative the ablative case is,
The Furies had most disagreeable faces.

Nouns declined with two articles, are called common. This word common requires explanation—it is not used in the same sense as that in which we say, that quackery is common in medicine, knavery in the law, and humbug everywhere—pigeons at Crockford's, lame ducks at the Stock Exchange, Jews at the ditto, and Royal ditto, and foreigners in Leicester Square—No; a common noun is one that is both masculine and feminine; in one sense of the word therefore it is *uncommon*. Parens, a parent, which may be declined both with hic, and hæc, is, for obvious reasons, a noun of this class; and so is fur, a thief; likewise miles, a soldier, which will appear strange to those of our readers, who do not call to mind the existence of the ancient amazons; the dashing white sergeant being the only female soldier known in modern times. Nor have we more than one authenticated instance of a female sailor, if we except the heroine commemorated in the somewhat apocryphal narrative—Billy Taylor.

Nouns are called doubtful when declined with the article hic or hæc—whichever you please, as the showman said of the Duke of Wellington and Napoleon Bonaparte. Anguis, a snake, is a doubtful noun. At all events he is a doubtful customer.

Epicene nouns are those which, though declined with one article only, represent both sexes, as hic passer, a sparrow, hæc aquila, an eagle,—cock and hen. A sparrow, however, to say nothing of an eagle, must appear a doubtful noun with regard to gender, to a cockney sportsman.

After all, there is no rule in the Latin language about gender so comprehensive as that observed in Hampshire, where they call every thing *he* but a tom-cat, and that *she.*

*   *   *   *   *

DECLENSION OF NOUNS SUBSTANTIVE.

There are five declensions of substantives. As a pig is known by his tail, so are declensions of substantives distinguished by the ending of the genitive case. Our fear of outraging the comic feelings of humanity, prevents us from saying quite so much about them as our love of learning would otherwise induce us to do. We therefore refer the student to that clever little book, the Eton Latin Grammar, strongly recommending him to decline the following substantives, by way of an exercise, after the manner of the examples there set down. First declension, Genitivo æ. Virga, a rod. —Second, i. Puer, a boy. Stultus, a fool. Tergum, a back. —Third, is. Vulpes, a fox. Procurator, an attorney. Cliens, a client. —Fourth, ûs— here you may have, Risus, a laugh at. —Fifth, ei. Effigies, an effigy, image, or Guy.

The substantive face, facies, *makes faces*, facies, in the plural.

Although we are precluded from going through the whole of the declensions, we cannot refrain from proposing "for the use of schools," a model upon which all substantives may be declined in a mode somewhat more agreeable, if not more instructive, than that heretofore adopted.

Exempli Gratiâ.

Musa mus*æ*,
The Gods were at tea,
Musæ mus*am.*
Eating raspberry jam,
Musa mus*â,*
Made by Cupid's mamma,
Musæ mus*arum,*
Thou "Diva Dearum."
Musis mus*as,*
Said Jove to his lass,
Musæ mus*is.*
Can ambrosia beat this?

*   *   *   *   *

DECLENSIONS OF NOUNS ADJECTIVE.

Some nouns adjective are declined with three terminations—as a pacha of three tails would be, if he were to make a proposal to an English heiress—as bonus, *good*—tener, *tender*. Sweet epithets! how forcibly they remind us of young Love and a leg of mutton.

> Bonus, bona, bonum,
> Thou little lambkin dumb,
> Boni, bonæ, boni,
> For those sweet chops I sigh,
> Bono, bonæ, bono,
> Have pity on my woe,
> Bonum, bonam, bonum,
> Thou speak'st though thou art mum,
> Bone, bona, bonum,
> "O come and eat me, come,"
> Bono, bonæ, bono,
> The butcher lays thee low,
> Boni, bonæ, bona,
> Those chops are a picture,—ah!
> Bonorum, bonarum, bonorum,
> To put lots of Tomata sauce o'er 'em
> Bonis—Don't, miss,
> Bonos, bonas, bona,
> Thou art sweeter than thy mamma,
> Boni, bonæ, bona,
> And fatter than thy papa.
> Bonis,—What bliss!

In like manner decline tener, tenera, tenerum.

Unus, one; solus, alone; totus, the whole; nullus, none; alter, the other; uter, whether of the two—make the genitive case singular in *ius* and the dative in i.

RIDDLES.

Q. In what case will a grain of barley joined to an adjective stand for the name of an animal?

A. In the dative case of unus—uni-corn.

> *Uni* nimirum tibi rectè semper erunt res.

Hor. Sat. lib. ii. 2. 106.

Q. Why is the above verse like all nature?

A. Because it is an *uni*-verse.

The word alius, another, is declined like the above-named adjectives, except that it makes ali*ud*, not ali*um*, in the neuter singular.

The difference of unus from alius, say the London commentators, like that of a humming-top from a peg-top, consists of the *'um*.

N.B. Tu es unus alius, is not good Latin for "You're another," a phrase more elegantly expressed by "Tu quoque."

TU QUOQUE.

There are some adjectives that remind us of lawyer's clerks, and, by courtesy, of linen-drapers' apprentices. These may be termed *articled* adjectives; being declined with the articles hic, hæc, hoc, after the third declension of substantives—as tristis, sad, melior, better, felix, happy.

It is not very easy to conceive any thing in which sadness and comicality are united, except Tristis Amator, a sad lover.

TRISTIS AMATOR.

Melior is not *better* for comic purposes. Felix affords no room for a *happy* joke.

Decline these three adjectives, and others of the same class, according to the following rules:

    If the nominative endeth in *is* or *er*, why, sir,
    The ablative singular endeth in *i*, sir;
    The first, fourth, and fifth case, their neuter make *e*,
    But the same in the plural in *ia* must be.
    E, or *i*, are the ablative's ends,—mark my song,
    While *or* to the nominative case doth belong;
    For the neuter aforesaid we settle it thus:
    The plural is *ora*; the singular *us*.
    If than *is*, *er*, and *or*, it hath many more enders,
    The nominative serves to express the three genders;
    But the plural for *ia* hath *icia* and *itia*,
    As Felix, felicia—Dives, divitia.

        *   *   *   *   *

COMPARISONS OF ADJECTIVES.

Comparisons are odious—

Adjectives have three degrees of comparison. This is perhaps the reason why they are so disagreeable to learn.

The first degree of comparison is the positive, which denotes the quality of a thing absolutely. Thus, the Eton Latin Grammar is lepidus, funny.

The second is the comparative, which increases or lessens the quality, formed by adding *or* to the first case of the positive ending in *i*. Thus the Charter House Grammar, is lepidor—funnier, or more funny. —The third is the superlative, which increases or diminishes the signification to the greatest degree, formed from the same case by adding thereto, *ssimus*. Thus the Comic Latin Grammar is lepidissimus, funniest, or most funny. A Londoner is acutus, sharp, or 'cute,—a Yorkshireman acutior, sharper, or more sharp, 'cuter or more 'cute—but a Yankee is acutissimus—sharpest, or most sharp, 'cutest or most 'cute, or tarnation 'cute.

Enumerate, in the manner following, with substantives, the exceptions to this rule, mentioned in the Eton Grammar.

Bonus, good.	Melior, better.	Optimus, best.
A plain pudding.	A suet pudding.	A plum pudding.
Malus, bad.	Pejor, worse.	Pessimus, worst.
A caning.	A spatting.	A flogging.

        &c. &c.

Adjectives ending in *er*, form the superlative in *errimus*. The taste of vinegar is acer, sour; that of verjuice acrior, more sour; the visage of a tee-totaller, acerrimus, sourest, or most sour.

Agilis, docilis, gracilis, facilis, humilis, similis, change *is* into *llimus*, in the superlative degree.

Agilis, nimble.—Madlle. Taglioni.
Agilior, more nimble.—Jim Crow.
Agillimus, most nimble.—Mr. Wieland.
Docilis, docile.—Learned Pig.
Docilior, more docile.—Ourang-outang.
Docillimus, most docile.—Man Friday.
Gracilis, slender.—A whipping post.
Gracilior, more slender.—A fashionable waist.
Gracillimus, most slender.—A dustman's leg.
&c. &c.

If a vowel comes before *us* in the nominative case of an adjective, the comparison is made by magis, *more*, and maximè, *most*.

Pius, pious.—Dr. Cantwell.
Magis pius, more pious.—Mr. Maw-worm.
Maximè pius, most pious.—Mr. Stiggins.

Sancho Panza called Don Quixote, Quixottissimus. This was not good Latin, but it evinced a knowledge on Sancho's part, of the nature of the superlative degree.

OF A PRONOUN.

A pronoun is a substitute, or (as we once heard a lady of the Malaprop family say), a *subterfuge* for a noun.

There are fifteen Pronouns.

Ego, tu, ille,
I, thou, and Billy,
Is, sui, ipse,
Got very tipsy.
Iste, hic, meus,
The governor did not see us.
Tuus, suus, noster,
We knock'd down a coster-
Vester, noster, vestras.
monger for daring to pester us.

To these may be added, egomet, I myself; tute, thou thyself, idem the same, qui, who or what, and cujas, of what country.

DECLENSION OF PRONOUNS.

Pronouns concern *ourselves* so much, that we cannot altogether pass over them; though a hint or two with regard to the mode of learning their declension is all that we can here afford to give. We are constrained now and then to leave out a good deal of valuable matter, for the reason that induced the Dublin manager to omit the part of Hamlet in the play of that name—the length of the performance.

Pronouns may be thus agreeably declined:

> Ego, mei, mihi,
> Hoist the frog up sky-high.
> Tu, tui, tibi,
> In Chancery they fib ye.
> Ille, illa, illud,
> Cows chew the cud.
> Is, ea, id,
> Always do as you're bid.
>
> Qui, quæ, quod,
> Or else you'll taste the rod.

Every donkey can decline is, ea, id. We heard one the other day on Hampstead Heath, repeat distinctly

E—o! e—a! e—o!

THE FIRST LESSON IN LATIN.

When you decline quis quæ *quid*, beware of any temptation to indulge in dirty habits. *E*schew pig-tail instead of chewing it. Never have any *quid* in your mouth, but a quid pro quo.

*　　　　*　　　　*　　　　*　　　　*

OF A VERB.

A verb is the chief word in every *sentence,* as *Suspendatur* per collum, let him be hanged by the neck.

It expresses the action or being of a thing. Ego *sum* sapiens, I am a wise man. Tu *es* stultus, thou art a fool. Non hic amice, *pernoctas,* you don't lodge here, Mr. Ferguson.

Verbs have two voices, like the gentleman who was singing, a short time since, at the St. James's Theatre.

The active ending in *o*—as amo, I love.

The passive ending in *or*—as amor, I am loved.

In these two words is contained the terrestrial summum bonum—In short, love beats everything—cock-fighting not excepted. Amo! amor! How happy every human being, from the peer to the pot-boy, from the duchess to the dairy-maid, would be to be able to say so.

They would *conjugate* immediately. Except, however, certain modern political economists of the Malthusian school, who, albeit they are great advocates for the diffusion of learning, are violently opposed to unlimited conjugations.

Of verbs ending in *o* some are actives transitive. A verb is called transitive when the action passes on to the following noun, as Seco baculum meum, I cut my stick.

Numerous examples of this kind of cutting, which may be called a *comic section,* are recorded in history, both ancient and modern. Even Hector cut his stick (with Achilles after him) at the siege of Troy. The Persians cut their stick at Marathon. Pompey cut his stick at Pharsalia, and so did Antony at Actium. Napoleon Bonaparte cut his stick at Waterloo.

Other verbs ending in *o* are named neuters and intransitives. A verb is called intransitive, or neuter, when the action does not pass on, or require a following noun, as curro, I run. Pistol cucurrit, Pistol ran. But to say, "Falstaff voluit *currere eum per,*" "Falstaff wished *to run him through,*" would be making a neuter verb, a verb active, and would therefore be Latin of the canine species, or Dog-Latin; so would Meus homo Gulielmus *cucurrit caput suum* plenum sed contra te homo dic pax, My man William *ran his head* full but against the mantel-piece. This, it is obvious, will not do after Cicero.

Verbs transitive ending in *o* become passive by changing *o* into *or,* as Secor, I am cut. Cæsar was cut by his friend Brutus in the capitol. "This," as Antony very judiciously observed on the hustings, "was the most unkindest *cut* of all,"—much worse, indeed, than any of the similar operations which are daily performed in Regent Street.

Verbs neuter and intransitive are never made passive. We may say, Crepo, I crack, but we cannot say, Crepor, I am cracked.

BRUTUS AND CÆSAR.

The ancient heroes appear, from what Homer says, to have got into a way of *cracking* away most tremendously when they were going to engage in single combat.

Orestes was certainly *cracked*.

Some verbs ending in *or* have an active signification—as Loquor, I speak.

Q. Why are such verbs like witnesses on oath?

A. Because they are called "Deponents."

Of these some few are neuters, as Glorior, I boast.

Cæsar boasted that he came, saw, and overcame. Bald-headed people (like Cæsar) do not, in general, make *conquests* so easily.

Neuter Verbs ending in *or*, and verbs deponent, are declined like verbs passive; but with gerunds and supines like verbs active; thus presenting a curious combination of *activity* and *supineness*.

There are some verbs which are called verbs personal. A verb personal resembles a mixed group of old maids and young maids, because it has *different persons*, as Ego irrideo, I quiz. Tu irrides, thou quizzest.

A verb impersonal is like a collection of tombstone angels, or small children; it has not *different persons*, as tædet, it irketh, oportet, it behoveth.

It irketh to learn Greek and Latin, nevertheless it behoveth to do so.

* * * * *

OF MOODS.

Moods in verbs are like moods in man, they have each of them a peculiar *expression*. Here, however, the resemblance stops. Man has many moods, verbs have but five. For instance, we observe in men the merry mood, the doleful mood, (or dumps), the shy, timid, or sheepish mood, the bold, or *bumptious* mood, the placid mood, the angry mood, whereto may be added the vindictive mood, and the sulky mood; the sober mood, as contradistinguished from both the serious and the drunken mood; or as blended with the latter, in which case it may be called the sober-drunk mood—the contented mood, the grumbling mood; the sympathetic mood, the sarcastic mood, the idle mood, the working mood, the communicative mood, the secretive mood, and the moods of all the phrenological organs; besides the monitory or mentorial mood, and the mendacious, or lying mood, with the imaginative, poetical, or romantic mood, the compassionate, or melting mood, and many other moods too tedious to mention.

A LONG COURTSHIP.

We must not however omit the flirting mood, the teazing or tantalizing mood, the giggling mood, the magging or talkative mood, and the scandalizing mood, which are peculiarly observable in the fair sex.

The moods of verbs are the following:

1. The indicative mood, which either affirms a fact or asks a question, as Ego amo, I *do* love. Amas tu? *Dost* thou love?

The long and short of all courtships are contained in these two examples.

2. The imperative mood, which commandeth, or entreateth. This two-fold character of the imperative mood is often exemplified in schools, the command being on the part of the master, and the entreaty on that of the boy—as thus, Veni huc! Come hither! Parce mihi! Spare me! The imperative mood is also known by the sign *let*—as in the well-known verse in the song Dulce Domum—

"Eja! nunc eamus."

"Hurrah! now let us be off"—meaning for the vacation. N.B. This mood is one much in the mouth of beadles, boatswains, bashaws, majors, magistrates, slave drivers, superintendents, serjeants, and jacks-in-office of all descriptions—monitors, especially, and præfects of public schools, are very fond of using it on all occasions.

THE IMPERATIVE MOOD.

3. The potential mood signifies power or duty. The signs by which it is known are, may, can, might, would, could, should, or ought—as, Amem, I may love (when I leave school). Amavissem, I should have loved (if I had not known better,) and the like.

4. The subjunctive differs from the potential only in being always governed by some conjunction or indefinite word, and in being subjoined to some other verb going before it in the same sentence—as Cochleare eram cum amarem, I was a *spoon* when I loved—Nescio qualis sim hoc ipso tempore, I don't know what sort of a person I am at this very time.

The propriety of the above expression "cochleare," will be explained in a Comic System of Rhetoric, which perhaps may appear hereafter.

5. The infinitive mood is like a gentleman's cab, because it has no number.

We have not made up our minds exactly, whether to compare it to the "picture of nobody" mentioned in the Tempest, or to the "picture of ugliness," which young ladies generally call their successful rivals. It may be like one, or the other, or both, because it has no *person*.

Neither has it a nominative case before it; nor, indeed, has it any more business with one than a toad has with a side pocket.

It is commonly known by the sign *to*. As, for example—Amare, to love; Desipere, to be a fool; Nubere, to marry; Pœnitere, to repent.

*   *   *   *   *

OF GERUNDS AND SUPINES.

Ever anxious to encourage the expansion of youthful minds, by as general a cultivation as possible of the various faculties, we beg to invite attention to the following combination of Grammar, Poetry, and Music.

Air.—Believe me if all those endearing young charms. —*Moore.*

The gerunds of verbs end in di, do, and dum,
But the supines of verbs are but two;
For instance, the active, which endeth in *um*,
And the passive which endeth in *u*.

Amandi, of loving, kind reader, beware;
Amando, in loving, be brief;
Amandum, to love, if you 're doom'd, have a care,
In the goblet to drown all your grief.

Amatum, Amatu, to love and be loved,
Should it be your felicitous (?) lot,
May the fuel so needful be never removed
Which serves to keep boiling the pot.

*   *   *   *   *

OF TENSES.

In verbs there are five tenses, or times, expressing an action, or affirmation.

1. The present tense, or time. There is no time (or tense) like the present. It expresses an action now taking place. Examples— *Act.* I love, or am loving. Amo, I am loving. —*Pass.* I am made drunk, or am drunk. Inebrior, I am drunk.

2. The preterimperfect tense denotes something, or a state of things, partly, but not entirely past. —Examp. I did love or was loving. Amabam, I was loving. I was made drunk an hour ago. Inebriabar, I was made drunk.

3. The preterperfect tense expresses a thing lately done, but now ended. —Examp. I have loved, or I loved. Amavi, I loved. I have been made drunk, or have been drunk. Inebriatus sum, I have been drunk.

4. The preterpluperfect tense refers to a thing done at some time past, but now ended. —Examp. Amaveram, I had loved. Inebriatus eram, I had been drunk.

5. The future tense relates to a thing to be done hereafter, as, Amabo, I shall or will love. Inebriabor, I shall get drunk—say to-morrow.

*   *   *   *   *

OF NUMBERS AND PERSONS.

Verbs have two numbers. No. 1, Singular, No. 2, Plural.

In most matters it is usual to pay exclusive attention to number one. In learning the verbs, however, it is necessary to regard equally number two.—The *persons* of verbs are generally considered very disagreeable. Verbs have three persons in each number. Thus, for instance, at a dancing academy—

Sing.	Ego salto,	I dance,
	Tu saltas,	Thou dancest,
	Ille saltat,	He danceth.
Plur.	Nos saltamus,	We dance,
	Vos saltatis,	Ye dance,
	Illi saltant,	They dance.

At an academy on *Free-knowledge-ical* principles—or a Comic Academy.

Ego rideo,	I laugh,
Tu rides,	Thou laughest,
Ille ridet,	He laugheth.
Nos ridemus,	We laugh,
Vos ridetis.	Ye laugh,
Illi rident,	They laugh.

Laughter, too, is very common at other academies, but generally occurs on the wrong side of the mouth. The right sort of laughter (which may be presumed to be on the *right* side of the mouth), is most frequent about the time of the holidays. What does the song say?

"Ridet annus, prata rident
Nosque rideamus."

"The year laughs, the meadows laugh,—suppose we have a laugh as well."

Note—That all nouns are of the third person except Ego, Nos, Tu, and Vos. Hence we see how absurdly the man who drew a couple of donkeys acted in endeavouring to prevail upon *us* to call the picture "*We* Three"—*Ille, he,*—may, perhaps, have been qualified to make a *third person* in the group, and have "written himself down an ass" with some correctness. *Ego, I,* and *Nos, we,* have certainly nothing in common with that animal, and it is to be hoped that neither Tu, thou, nor Vos, ye, can be said to partake of his nature.

Note also. That all nouns of the vocative case are of the second person. So that if we should say, O asine, O thou donkey; or O asini, O ye donkeys, we should have grammar at least on our side.

Be it your care to prevent us from having justice also.

OF THE VERB ESSE, TO BE.

Before other verbs are declined, it is necessary to learn the verb Esse, to be. And before we teach the verb Esse, to be, it is necessary to make a few remarks on verbs in general.

In the first place we have to observe, that they are rather difficult; and in the next, that if any one expects that we are going to consider them in detail, he is very much mistaken.

But our skipping a very considerable portion of the verbs, is no reason why boys should do the same. Were we all to follow the examples of our teachers, instead of attending to their precepts, where would be the world by this time?

Whirling away, no doubt, far from the respectable society of the neighbouring planets, and blundering about right and left, pell-mell, helter-skelter among the fixed stars—itself, "and all which it inherit" in that glorious state of confusion so admirably described by the poet Ovid—

"Quem dixere Chaos,"

which men have called Shaos. It would indeed be little better than a broken down *Shay*-horse.

But "revenons à nos moutons," that is, let us get back to our verbs. We recommend the most attentive and diligent study of all of them as set forth in the Eton Grammar, assisted by that kind of association of ideas, of which we shall now proceed to give a few specimens.

Sum, es, fui, esse, futurus, to be,—or not to be—that is the question.

Rule 1. To each person of a verb, singular and plural, join a noun, according to your taste or comic talent. Should you be deficient in the inventive faculty, apply for assistance to one of the senior boys, which, in consideration of your fagging for him, he will readily give you. If yourself a senior boy, apply to the master.

Examples.

INDICATIVE MOOD.

Present Tense. Am.

Sing.

Sum,	I am,	Vir,	a man,
Es,	Thou art,	Stultus,	a fool,
Est,	He is,	Latro,	a thief.

Plu.

Sumus,	We are,	Patricii,	gentlemen,
Estis,	Ye are,	Plebeii,	snobs,
Sunt,	They are,	Errones,	vagabonds.

We would proceed in this way with Sum, but that we are afraid of being tire-*sum.*

VERBS REGULAR.

First Conjugation. Amo.

Sing.

Amo,	I love,	Puellam,	a lass,
Amas,	Thou lovest,	Fartum,	a pudding,
Amat,	He loveth,	Carnem porcinam,	pork.

Plu.

Amamus,	We love,	Doctrinam,	learning,
Amatis,	Ye love,	Leporem,	comicality,
Amant,	They love,	Poesin,	poetry.

The consideration of which three things leads us to

Rule 2. In repeating the different tenses of verbs, be careful to be provided with a short English verse, contrived so as to rhyme with the third person singular, and another to rhyme with the third person plural. In this way your powers of composition as well as of memory will be profitably exercised.

Example.

Second Conjugation. Moneo.

Sing.　　Moneo, mones, monet,
　　　　　　Reid & Co.'s *heavy wet.*

Plu.　　Monemus, monetis, monent,
　　　　　　Beats that from the firmament.

Third Conjugation. Rego.

Sing.　　Rego, regis, regit,
　　　　　　A statesman for office unfit.

Plu.   Regimus, regitis, re*gunt*,
            Is much like a bear in a punt.

Rule 3. Should you be desired to give the English of each person in the tense which you are repeating, you may (we mean a class of you), follow a plan adopted with great success and striking effect in that kind of dramatic representation entitled "A Grand Opera," that of *singing* what you have to *say*. Hold up your head, turn out your toes, clear your voices, and begin. A-hem!

SCHOOLMASTER BEATING A DRUM, AND BOYS SINGING IN CHORUS.

Going through the Verbs. Audio—I Hear.

Fourth Conjugation. Audio.

Trio.

Sing. Audio,   I hear the Tartar drum!
        Audis,   Thou hearest the Tartar drum!
        Audit,   He hears the Tartar drum!—the Tartar
                 drum! the Tartar drum!

        Chorus.   He hears!
                    He hears!

He h - - e - - - a - - rs the Tar - tar drum!

Plu.   Audimus, We hear the Tartar drum, &c.

Verbs Irregular—

Are *regular* bores. The above Rules are equally applicable to them, and also to the

Defective Verbs;

Concerning which it may be asserted, that though almost all of them have tenses more or less imperfect, there are some which have not a single *Imperfect Tense.*

PRETTY DEAR.

IMPERSONAL VERBS.

Such as delectat, it delighteth; decet, it becometh, &c., answer to such English verbs as take the word *it* before them. When we consider that *it* is a term of endearment used in speaking to babies, as "it's a pretty dear," we cannot help thinking that Verbs Impersonal ought to be *pet* verbs. Such however, is not, as far as we know, the fact.

*   *   *   *   *

OF A PARTICIPLE.

A participle is a hybrid part of speech; a kind of mongrel-cross, between a noun and a verb. It is two parts verbs, and four parts noun; wherefore its composition may be likened unto the milk sold in and about London, which is usually watered in the proportion of four to two. The properties of the noun belonging to it, are, number, gender, case, and declension; those of the verb, tense, and signification.

As a horse hath four legs, so hath a verb four participles.

Air.—Bonnets of Blue.

There 's one of the present,—and then,
There 's one of the future in *rus*;
Of the tense preterperfect a third,—and again,
A fourth of the future in *dus*.

Participles are declined like nouns adjective, as—but no! how can we ask our fair (blue) readers to decline *a-man's* (amans) loving.

Now here we feel called upon to say a few words on the difference between a man's loving and a woman's loving. It has often been a question, whether do men or women love most *dearly*? To us the matter does not appear to admit of a doubt. We defy any of our male readers to be in love (when they are old and silly enough) for six months without finding themselves most grievously out of pocket. We have a friend who was in that unfortunate condition for about a month, and it cost him at least seven and sixpence a week in fees to the maid servant, and that without once being enabled to exchange a word with the object of his affections. At last he began to think that he was paying rather too dear for his whistle; so he gave it up. What girl would have held on so long, and laid out so much money without a return— not of soft affection, but of hard cash? Women, indeed, instead of loving dearly, love, according to our own experience, particularly cheaply. Think of what they save, by taking their admirers "shopping" with them, in ribands, bracelets, and the like, to say nothing of coach-hire, pastry-cooks, and the price of admission, when they go with them to the play. And we should like to hear of the young lady who in these days would dispose of her hand at any thing less than a good round sum if she could help it—no, no. To love *dearly* is the precious prerogative of the lords of the creation alone.

But we are forgetting our participles.

The participle of the present tense ends in *ans*, or *ens*; as Flagellans, whipping;

Lædens, hurting.

That of the future in *rus*, signifies a likelihood, or design of doing something, as Flagellaturus, about to whip; Læsurus, about to hurt.

That of the preterperfect tense has generally a passive signification, and ends in *us*, as Flagellatus, whipped; Læsus, hurt.

That of the future in *dus* has also a passive signification, as Flagellandus, to be whipped; Lædendus, to be hurt.

Note 1. All participles are declined like nouns adjective. We recommend the above participles to be declined like *winking*.

2. There are three things that are not hurt by whipping—a top, a syllabub, and a cream.

*   *   *   *   *

OF AN ADVERB.

Convex and concave spectacles are contrivances used to increase or diminish the magnitude of objects.

Adverbs are parts of speech used to increase or diminish the signification of words.

Spectacles are joined to the bridge of the nose.

Adverbs are joined to nouns adjective, and verbs. Benè, well; multùm, much; malè, ill, &c. are adverbs.

> Cæsar *multûm* conturbavit indigenas:
> Cæsar much astonished the natives.

CÆSAR ASTONISHING THE NATIVES.

*   *   *   *   *

OF A CONJUNCTION.

A conjunction is a part of speech that joineth together; wherefore it may be likened unto many things; for instance—

To glue, to paste, to gum arabic, to mortar, (for it joins words and sentences together *like bricks*), to Roman cement, (*Latin* conjunctions more especially), to white of egg, to isinglass, to putty, to adhesive plaster, to matrimony.

Conjunctions are thus used.

Ova *et* lardum, eggs and bacon. Dimidium dimidium*que*, half-and-half. Amor *et* dementia, love and madness.

HALF-AND-HALF.

*   *   *   *   *

OF A PREPOSITION.

A Preposition is a part of speech commonly *set before* another word. Words, however, do not eat each other, though men have been known to eat words. Ab, ad, ante, &c. prepositions.

Sometimes a preposition is joined in composition with another word, as *pros*tratus, knocked down—floored.

Tullius ab aquario *pros*tratus est:
Tully was knocked down by a waterman.

*   *   *   *   *

OF AN INTERJECTION.

An interjection is a word expressing a sudden emotion or feeling, as Hei! Oh dear!—Heu! Lack-a-day!—Hem! Brute, Hollo! Brutus.—Euge! Tite, Bravo! Titus.

We here find ourselves approaching the delightful subject of the three Concords, with which we shall make short work, first, for fear of further *Accidence*, and, secondly, because we are no fonder than boys are of *repetitions*, which, were we to follow the Eton Grammar in the Concords, we should be obliged to make in the Syntax.

However, there are just one or two points to be mentioned.

Rule. (Text-hand copy-books.) "Ask no questions."

Exception. When you want to find where the concord should be, ask the following—

Who? or what?—to find the nominative case to the verb.

Whom? or what? with the verb, for the accusative after it.

Who? or what? with the adjective, for the substantive to the adjective.

Who? or what? with the verb, for the antecedent to the relative.

But remember, that the use of the interrogatives who? and what? however justifiable in grammar, is very impertinent in conversation. What, for example, can be more ill-bred than to say, Who are you? Indeed, most questions are ill mannered. We do not speak of such expressions as, Has your mother sold her mangle? and the like, used only by persons who have never asked themselves where they expect to go to? but of all unnecessary demands whatever. "Sir," said the great Dr. Johnson, "it is uncivil to be continually asking, Why is a dog's tail short, or why is a cow's tail long."

*   *   *   *   *

OF THE GENDERS OF NOUNS,

Commonly known by the name of

"Propria Quæ Maribus."

As the "Propria Quæ Maribus" is no joke, and the "As in Præsenti" is too much of a joke, we must do with them as we did with the verbs. Singing a song is always esteemed a valid substitute for telling a story; and the indulgence which we would have extended to us in this respect, is that universally granted to civilized society.

Let the "Propria Quæ Maribus" be turned into a series of exercises, thus, or in like manner—

Air.—"Here 's to the maiden of bashful fifteen."

All names of the male kind you masculine call,
Ut sunt (for example), Divorum,
Mars, Bacchus, Apollo, the deities all,
And Cato, Virgilius, virorum.

Latin 's a bore, and bothers me sore,
Oh how I wish that my lesson was o'er.

Fluviorum, ut Tibris, Orontes likewise,
Fine rivers in ocean that lost are,
And Mensium—October an instance supplies;
Ventorum, ut Libs, Notus, Auster.
Latin 's a bore, &c.

We do not pretend that the mode of study here recommended, is perfectly original. The genuine Propria Quæ Maribus, and As in Præsenti, like the writings of the most remote antiquity, consist of certain useful truths recorded in harmonious numbers. It has been a question among commentators, whether these interesting compositions were originally intended to be said or sung. Analogy (we mean that derived from the works of Homer and Virgil) would incline us to the latter opinion, which however does not appear to have been generally entertained in the schools. We shall give one more specimen in the above style; and we beg it may be remembered, that in so doing, we have no wish to detract in any way from the merit of the illustrious poet in the Eton Grammar; all we think is, that he might have introduced a little more *comicality* into his work, while he was about it.

*   *   *   *   *

OF THE PRETERPERFECT TENSE, &C. OF VERBS.

Otherwise the "As in Præsenti."

As in Præsenti—Preterperfect—avi,
Oh! send me well done, lean, and lots of gravy,
Save lavo, lavi, nexo, nexui.
Ah! me—how sweet is cream with apple-pie,
Juvi from juvo, secui from seco,
Could n't I lie and tipple, more Græco!
From neco, necui, and mico, word
Which micui makes, Oh! roast goose, lovely bird!
Plico which plicui gives. Delightful grub!
And frico, fricas, fricui, to rub—
So domo, tono, domui, tonui make.
And sono, sonui.—Lead me to the stake,
I mean the beef-*stake*—crepo, crepui too,
Which means to *crack* (as roasted chestnuts do,)
Then veto, vetui makes—*forbidding* sound,
Cubo, to lie along (these verbs confound
Ye gods) makes cubui, do gives rightly dedi;
What viler object than a coat that 's seedy?—
Sto to form steti has a predilection;
Well—let it if it likes, I've no objection.
&c. &c. &c.

*   *   *   *   *

SYNTAXIS,

or the Construction of Grammar.

Q. What part of the grammar resembles the indulgences sold in the middle ages?

A. Sin-tax.

*   *   *   *   *

THE FIRST CONCORD;
THE NOMINATIVE CASE AND THE VERB.

Where there is much *personality*, there is generally little concord.

However, a verb personal agrees with its nominative case in number and person, as Sera nunquam est ad bonos mores via, The way to good manners is never too late. Mind that, brother Jonathan.

AMERICAN GENTLEMEN.

Note—The above maxim is especially worthy of the attention of neophytes in law and medicine; of the gods in the gallery, and of Members of the *House.*

The nominative case of pronouns is rarely expressed, except for the sake of distinction or emphasis, as—

Tu es exquisitus, *tu* es,
You 're a nice man, *you* are.

INGENUAS PUGNI DIDICISSE FIDELITER ARTES MOLLITOS MORES NON SINIT ESSE VIRI (FIGHT).

Sometimes a sentence is the nominative case to the verb, as

Ingenuas pugni didicisse fideliter artes,
Mollitos mores non sinit esse viri.

The faithful study of the fistic art
From mawkish softness guards a Briton's heart.

Who can doubt it? But, besides, we have much to say in praise of boxing. In the
first place, it is a *classical* accomplishment. To say nothing of the Olympic and Isth-

mian Games, which are of themselves sufficient proof of the elegant and *fanciful* tastes of the ancients; we need only allude to the fact, that the *Corinthians* are universally celebrated for their proficiency in this science. Then, of its eminently *social* tendency, there can be no doubt. What can be more conducive to good fellowship, and conviviality than the frequent *tapping of claret,* attendant both on its study and practice? Nor can its beneficial influence on the fine arts be called in question, seeing that its immediate object is to teach us the *use of our hands.* And (which perhaps is the most pursuasive argument of all), it is particularly pleasing to the fair sex, who besides their well known admiration of *bravery*, are, to a woman, devotedly attached to the *ring*.

Sometimes an adverb with a genitive case stands in the place of the nominative, as—

> Partim astutorum mordebantur,
> Part of the knowing ones were bit.

We must contend that the above is a *racy* observation.

EXCEPTIONS TO THE RULE.

Verbs of the infinitive mood—but hold. Remember that there is scarcely any rule without an exception; and this axiom particularly applies to the Syntax. We used to wish it did not; because then we should not have had so much to learn—to resume however—

Verbs of the infinitive mood often have set before them an accusative case instead of a nominative; the conjunction quod, or ut, being left out, as

> Annam reginam aiunt occubuisse:
> They say that Queen Anne's dead.

A verb placed between two nominative cases of different numbers, is not like a donkey between two stacks of hay, it makes choice of one or the other, and agrees with it, as

> Amygdalæ amaræ venenum *est,*
> Bitter almonds *is* poison.

We have written the English beneath the Latin. Perhaps it may be imagined that we think good English *beneath* us.

A singular noun of multitude is sometimes joined to a plural verb; as

Pars puerorum philosophum secuti sunt,
Part of the boys followed the philosopher.

And so they would now, particularly if they saw one in costume.

Verbs impersonal have no nominative case before them, as

Tædet me Grammatices, I am weary of Grammar.
Pertæsum est Syntaxeos, I am quite sick of Syntax.
Mirificum visum est Socratem in gyrum saltantem videre,
It seemed wonderful to behold Socrates jumping Jim Crow.

SECOND CONCORD.
THE SUBSTANTIVE AND THE ADJECTIVE.

A TEA SPOON.

Adjectives, participles, and pronouns agree with the substantive in gender, number, and case, as

Vir exiguo conventui, sobrioque idoneus:
A nice man for a small tea-party.

The Spartans, probably, were men of this kind; their aversion to drunkenness being well known.

Observe how close the concord is between substantive and adjective. The ties of wedlock are nothing to it; for, besides that in that happy state there is very often not a little discord, it is quite impossible that man and wife should ever agree in *gender*.

Sometimes a sentence supplies the place of a substantive; the adjective being placed in the neuter gender, as

Audito reginam leones cœnantes visisse:
It being heard that Her Majesty had gone to see the lions at supper.

Third Concord.
The relative and the antecedent.

The relative and antecedent hit it off very well together; they agree one with the other in gender, number, and person, as

Qui plenos haurit cyathos, madidusque quiescit,
Ille bonam degit vitam, moriturque facetus.
"He who drinks plenty, and goes to bed mellow,
Lives as he ought to do, and dies a jolly fellow."

Horace was the fellow for this kind of thing. Cato must have been a regular wet blanket.

HELIOGABALUS.

Sometimes a sentence is placed for an antecedent, as

> Heliogabalus, spiritu contento, viginti quatuor ostrearum demersit in alvum, quod Dandoni etiam longé antecellit.
> Heliogabalus, at one breath, swallowed two dozen of oysters, which beats even Dando out and out.

Many of the ancients could swallow a good deal.

A relative placed between two substantives of different genders and numbers, sometimes agrees with the latter, as

> Pueri tuentur illum librum quæ Latina Grammatices et Comica dicitur.
> Boys regard that book which is called the Comic Latin Grammar.

Sometimes a relative agrees with the primitive, which is understood in the possessive, as

> Mirabantur impudentiam suam qui ad reginam literas misit.
> They wondered at his impudence, who wrote a letter to the queen.

If a nominative case be interposed between the relative and the verb, the relative is governed by the verb, or by some other word which is placed in the sentence with the verb, as

> Luciferi quos Prometheus surripuit, ad Jovem cujus numen contempsit, pertinebant.
> The Lucifers which Prometheus shirked, belonged to Jupiter, whose authority he despised.

In fact, Prometheus *made light* of Jupiter's *lightning*.

We now take leave of the Concords, observing only how pleasant it is to see *relatives agree*.

IT 'S PLEASANT TO SEE RELATIVES AGREE.

PROMETHEUS VINCTUS (VAGABOND IN THE STOCKS).

Our next subject is the

Construction of Nouns Substantive.

Which is not quite so amusing as the construction of small boats, paper kites, pinwheels, crackers, or any other mode of displaying the faculty of "constructiveness"—though in one sense the construction of nouns substantive, is not unlike the construction of *puzzles*.

When two substantives of a different signification meet together, the latter is put in the genitive case, as

> Ulysses lumen Cyclopis extinxit:
> Ulysses doused the glim of the Cyclops.

This genitive case is sometimes changed into a dative, as

> Urbi pater est, urbique maritus. —Gram. Eton.
> He is the father of the city, and the husband of the city.

He must have been a pretty fellow, whoever he was.

An adjective of the neuter gender, put without a substantive, sometimes requires a genitive case, as

> Paululùm honestatis sartori sufficit:
> A very little honesty is enough for a tailor.

A genitive case is sometimes placed alone; the preceding substantive being understood by the figure ellipsis, as

> Ubi ad magistri veneris, cave verbum de porco:
> When you are come to the master's (house), not a word about the pig.

The word pig is a very general term, and is used to signify not only the animal so called, and such of the human race as resemble him in habits, appearance, or feelings; but also to denote a variety of little things, which it is sometimes necessary to keep secret. A pedagogue now and then discovers a *pig-tail* appended to his coat collar—this, or rather the way in which it got there, is one of the little *pigs* in question. Robbing the larder or the garden is another; so is insinuating horsehairs into the cane, or putting cobbler's wax on the seat of learning —we mean the master's stool. A sort of *pig* (or rather a *rat*) is sometimes *smelt* by the master on taking his nightly walk though the dormitories, when roast fowl, mince pies, bread and cheese, shrub, punch, &c. have been slyly smuggled into those places of repose. Shirking down town is always a *pig*, and the consequences thereof, in case of discovery, a great *bore*.

Considering that a secret is a *pig*, it is singular that betraying one should be called letting the *cat* out of the bag.

Two substantives respecting the same thing are put in the same case, as

> Telemachum, juvenem bonæ indolis, Calypso existimavit.
> Calypso thought Telemachus a nice young man.

By the way, what a nice young man Virgil makes out Marcellus to have been!

SMELLING A PIG (BOYS AT SUPPER IN THE BED ROOM).

Praise, dispraise, or the quality of a thing is placed in the ablative, and also in the genitive case—as

> Vir paucorum verborum et magni appetitûs:
> A man of few words and large appetite.
> Paterfamilias. Vir multis miseriis:
> A father of a family. A man of many woes.

The man of most *woes*, however, is a hackney-coachman.

Opus, need, and usus, need, require an ablative case, as

> Didoni marito opus erat;
> Dido had need of a husband.
> Æneæ cœnâ usus erat;
> Æneas had need of a dinner.

But opus appears to be sometimes placed like an adjective for necessarius, necessary, as

> Regi Anthropophagorum coquus opus est:
> The King of the Cannibal Islands wants a cook.

Which would serve his purpose best—a valet-de-chambre who *dresses* men, or a wit, who *roasts* them?

THE CONSTRUCTION OF NOUNS ADJECTIVE.
THE GENITIVE CASE AFTER THE ADJECTIVE.

Adjectives which signify desire, knowledge, memory, fear, and the contrary to these, require a genitive case, as

> Est natura vetularum obtrectationis avida:
> The nature of old women is fond of scandal.

This particularly applies to old maids. As those delightful creatures now-a-days, not content with being *grey* aspire to be actually *blue*; we cannot help recommending to them a kind of study, for which their propensity to *cutting up* renders them peculiarly adapted; we mean *Anatomy*. And since it is on the foulest and most odious points of character that they chiefly delight to dwell, we more especially suggest to them the pursuit of *Morbid Anatomy,* as one which is likely to be attended both with gratification and success.

> Mens tempestatum præscia:
> A mind foreknowing the weather.

A piece of *sea-weed* has often, heretofore, been used as a barometer; but it is only of late that this purpose has been answered by a *murphy.*

> Immemor beneficii:
> Unmindful of a kindness.

The sort of kindness one is least likely to forget is that which our master used to say he conferred upon us, when he was inculcating learning by means of the rod. We cannot help thinking, however, that he began *at the wrong end.*

> Imperitus rerum:
> Unacquainted with the world, i.e. Not 'up to snuff'.

Much controversy has been wasted in attempts to determine the origin of the phrase "up to snuff". Some have contended that it was suggested by the well-known quality possessed by snuff, of *clearing the head*; but this idea is far fetched, not to say absurd. Others will have that the expression was derived from Snofe, or Snoffe, the name of a cunning rogue who flourished about the time of the first crusade; so that "up to Snoffe" signified as clever, or knowing, as Snoffe; and was in process of time converted into "up to snuff." This opinion is deserving of notice; though the only argument in its favour is, that the phrase in question was in vogue long before the discovery of tobacco. Probably the soundest view is that which connects it with the proper name Znoufe, which in ancient High-Dutch is equivalent to Mercury, whose reputation for astuteness among the ancients was exceedingly great. Conf. Hookey-Walk, ii. 13. Hok. Pok. Wonk-Fum. viii. 24. Cheek. Marin. passim, with a host of commentators, ancient and modern.

> Roscius timidus Deorum fuit:
> *Roscius* was afraid of the *Gods.*

Adjectives ending in *ax,* derived from verbs, also require a genitive case, as

> Tempus edax rerum:
> Time is the consumer of all things.

Hence Time is sometimes figured as an alderman.

Nouns partitive, nouns of number, nouns comparative and superlative, and certain adjectives put partitively, require a genitive case, from which also they take their gender; as

> Utrum horum mavis accipe:
> Take which of those two things you had rather.

So Queen Eleanor gave Fair Rosamond her choice between the dagger and the bowl of poison. This, to our mind, would have been like choosing a tree to be hanged on.

> Primus fidicinum fuit Orpheus:

Orpheus was the first of fiddlers.

He is said to have charmed the hearts of broomsticks.

> Momus lepidissimus erat Deorum:
> Momus was the funniest of the Gods.

Other deities may have made Jupiter shake his head. Momus used to make him shake his sides.

> Sequimur te, sancte deorum:
> We follow thee, O sacred deity.

Namely, the aforesaid Momus. He is the only heathen god that we should have had much reverence for, and certainly the only one that we should ever have sacrificed to at all. The offering most commonly made to the god of laughter was, probably, *a sacrifice of propriety.*

But the above nouns are also used with these prepositions, a, ab, de, e, ex, inter, ante; as,

> Primus inter philosophos Democritus est:
> Democritus is the first amongst philosophers.

And why? Because he alone was wise enough to find out that laughing is better than crying. He it was who first proved to the world that philosophy and comicality are, in fact, one science; and that the more we learn the more we laugh. We forget whether it was he or Aristotle who made the remark, that man is the only laughing animal except the hyæna.

Secundus sometimes requires a dative case, as

> Haud ulli veterum virtute secundus:
> Inferior to none of the ancients in valour.

Surely Virgil in saying this, had an eye to a hero, whose fame has been perpetuated in the verses of a later poet.

"Some talk of Alexander, and some of Pericles,

Of Conon and Lysander, and Alcibiades;
But of all the gallant heroes, there 's none for to compare,
With my ri-fol-de-riddle-iddle-lol to the British grenadier!"

An interrogative, and the word which answers to it, shall be of the same case and tense, except words of a different construction be made use of; as

Quarum rerum nulla est satietas? Pomorum.
Of what things is there no fulness? Of fruit.

Dr. Johnson used to say that he never got as much wall fruit as he could eat.

THE DATIVE CASE AFTER THE ADJECTIVE.

Adjectives by which advantage, disadvantage, likeness, unlikeness, pleasure, submission, or relation to any thing is signified, require a dative case; as

Astaci incocti patriæ idonei sunt in pace; cocti autem in bello.
Raw lobsters are serviceable to their country in peace; but boiled ones in war. Lobster's *claws* are nasty things to get into.

The Corporation of London seemed very much afraid of the *Police clause*.

One of the reasons why a soldier is sometimes called a lobster, probably is, that the latter is a *marine* animal.

Balænæ persimile:
Very like a whale.

Qui color albus erat nunc est contrarius albo:
The colour which was white is now contrary to white.

Some people will swear white is black to gain their ends; and a man who will do this, though he may not always be—

Jucundus amicis:
Pleasant to his friends;

is nevertheless frequently so to his *constituents*.

Hither are referred nouns compounded of the preposition *con*, as contubernalis, a comrade; commilito, a fellow soldier, &c. You must *con* all such words attentively before you can *con*strue well, or the *con*sequence will be, that you will be *con*siderably blown up, if not *con*foundedly flogged.

Some of these which signify similitude, are also joined to a genitive case, as

> Par uncti fulminis:
> Like greased lightning.

The familiarity of our transatlantic friends with the nature of the electric fluid, is no doubt owing to the discoveries of their countryman Franklin. *Q.* Was the lightning which that philosopher drew down from the clouds, of the kind mentioned in the example?

Communis, common; alienus, strange; immunis, free, are joined to a genitive, dative, and also to an ablative case, with a preposition, as

> Aures longæ communes asinorum sunt:
> Long ears are common to asses.

Though *musical* ears are not. We even doubt whether they would have the slightest admiration for *Bray*-ham.

> Non sunt communes caudæ hominibus:
> Tails are not common to men.

Except coat-tails, shirt-tails, pig-tails, and rats'-tails—to which en-*tails* may perhaps also be added, though these last are often cut off.

> Non alienus a poculo cerevisiæ:
> Not averse to a pot of beer.

We should think we were not; and should as soon think of engaging in an unnatural quarrel with our bread and butter.

Natus, born; commodus, convenient; incommodus, inconvenient; utilis, useful; inutilis, useless; vehemens, earnest; aptus, fit, are sometimes also joined to an accusative case with a preposition, as

> Natus ad laqueum:
> Born to a halter.

Those who are reserved for this exalted destiny, are said to enjoy a peculiar immunity from drowning. Is this the reason why *watermen* are such a set of rogues?

To prevent mistakes, it should be mentioned, that the *watermen* here meant are those who, by their own account, are so called from their office being *to shut the doors of hackney coaches*.

Verbal adjectives ending in *bilis*, taken passively, and participles made adjectives ending in *dus*, require a dative case; as

> Nulli penetrabilis astro;
> Penetrable by no *star*— not fond of *acting*?
> O venerande mihi Liston! te luget Olympus:
> O Liston, to be venerated by me the *Olympic* bewails thee.

The Accusative Case after the Adjective.

The measure of quantity is put after adjectives, in the accusative, the ablative, and the genitive case, as

> Anguis centum pedes longus:
> A snake a hundred feet long.
> Arbor gummifera, alta mille et quingentis passibus.
> A gum-tree a mile and a half high.
> Aranea, lata pedum denum:
> A spider ten feet broad.

An accusative case is sometimes put after adjectives and participles, where the preposition secundum, appears to be understood, as

> Os humerosque asello similis:
> Like to a cod-fish as to his head and shoulders.

Some men *are* exceedingly like a cod-fish, as to their head and shoulders, and they often endeavour to increase this natural resemblance as much as possible, by wearing *gills*.

The Ablative Case after the Adjective.

Adjectives which relate to plenty or want, sometimes require an ablative, sometimes a genitive case, as

> Amor et melle et felle est fœcundissimus:
> Love is very full both of honey and gall.

The *honey* of love is—we do not know exactly what. Honey, however, is Latin for love, as the Irishman said.

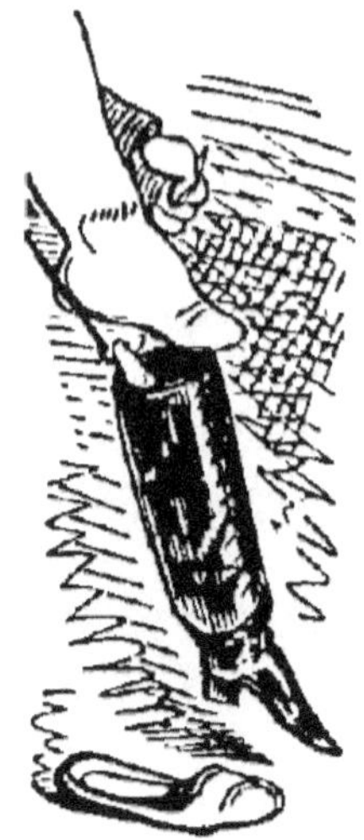

A TIGHT BOOT.

The gall of love consists in

First. Tight boots, in which it is often necessary to do penance before *our Lady's* window. This is at all events very *galling*.

Secondly. In lover's sighs, to which it communicates their peculiar *bitterness*.

Thirdly. Another very *galling* thing in love is being cut out.

Fourthly. Love is one of the passions treated of by *Gall* and Spurzheim.

Adjectives and substantives govern an ablative case, signifying the cause and the form, or the manner of a thing, as

> Demosthenes vociferatione raucus erat:
> Demosthenes was hoarse with bawling.

> Nomine grammaticus, re barbarus:
> A grammarian in name; in reality a barbarian.

Like many of the old masters—we do not mean painters—though we certainly allude to *brothers of the brush*—perhaps it would be better to call them *brothers of the angle*, on account of their partiality to the *rod*. Does the reader *twig*? If so, it is unnecessary to *branch* out into a discussion with regard to the nature of the barbarity hinted at—a kind of barbarity which, though it may proclaim its perpetrators to be by no means allied to the *feline* race, connects them most decidedly with the *canine* species.

Dignus, worthy; indignus, unworthy; præditus, endued; captus, disabled; contentus, content; extorris, banished; fretus, relying upon; liber, free; with adjectives signifying price, require an ablative case, as

> Leander dignus erat meliore fato:
> Leander was worthy of a better fate.

Poor fellow! first to be head over ears in love, and then over head and ears in the sea! Shocking! What an *hero*ic young man he must have been.—What *a duck*, too, the fair Hero must have thought him as she watched him from her lonely tower, nearing her every moment, as he cleft with lusty arm the foaming herring-pond. We mean the Hellespont—but no matter. What a *goose* he must have been considered by any one else who happened to know of his nightly exploits! How miserably he was *gulled* at last! Never mind. If Leander went to the *fishes* for love, many a better man than he, has, before and since, gone, from the same cause, to the *dogs*.

> Conscientia procuratoris solidis sex, denariis octo, venale est;
> A lawyer's conscience is to be sold for six and eightpence.

Some of these, sometimes admit a genitive case, as

> Carmina digna deæ:
> Verses worthy of a goddess.

Whether the following verses are worthy of a goddess or not, we shall not attempt to decide; they were addressed to one at all events—at least to a being who, if *idolizing* constitutes a goddess, may, perhaps, be termed one. We met with them in turning over the pages of an album.

LINES BY A FOND LOVER.

> Lovely maid, with rapture swelling,
> Should these pages meet thine eye,
> Clouds of absence soft dispelling;
> Vacant memory heaves a sigh.

> As the rose, with fragrance weeping,
> Trembles to the tuneful wave,
> So my heart shall twine unsleeping,
> Till it canopies the grave!

AN ALBUM AUTHOR.

> Though another's smiles requited,
> Envious fate my doom should be:
> Joy for ever disunited,
> Think, ah! think, at times on me!
>
> Oft amid the spicy gloaming,
> Where the brakes their songs instil,
> Fond affection silent roaming,
> Loves to linger by the rill—
>
> There when echo's voice consoling,
> Hears the nightingale complain,
> Gentle sighs my lips controlling,
> Bind my soul in beauty's chain.
>
> Oft in slumber's deep recesses,
> I thy mirror'd image see;
> Fancy mocks the vain caresses
> I would lavish like a bee!
>
> But how vain is glittering sadness!
> Hark, I hear distraction's knell!
> Torture gilds my heart with madness!
> Now for ever fare thee well!

It would be interesting as well as instructive to settle the difference between love verses and nonsense verses, if this were the proper place for doing so. But we are not yet come to the Prosody; nor shall we arrive there very soon unless we get on with the Syntax.

Comparatives, when they may be explained by the word quam, than, require an ablative case, as

> Achilles Agamemnone velocior erat:
> Achilles was a faster man than Agamemnon.

Fast men in modern times are very apt to *outrun the constable.*

Tanto, by so much, quanto, by how much, hoc, by this, eo, by this, and quo, by which; with some other words which signify the measure of exceeding; likewise ætate, by age, and natu, by birth, are often joined to comparatives and superlatives, as

> Tanto deformissimus, quanto sapientissimus philosophorum.
> By so much the ugliest, by how much the wisest of philosophers.

Such an one was Socrates. It is all very well to have a contemplative disposition; but it need not be accompanied by a *contemplative nose.*

> Quo plus habent, eo plus cupiunt:
> The more they have the more they want.

This is a curious fact in the natural history of school-boys, considered in relation to roast beef and plum pudding.

Maximum ætate virum in totâ Kentuckiâ contudi:
I whopped the oldest man in all Kentucky.

THE CONSTRUCTION OF PRONOUNS.

All those who would understand the construction of pronouns, should take care to be well versed in the distinction between *meum* and *tuum*, ignorance of which often gives rise to the disagreeable necessity of becoming too intimately acquainted with *quod*.

Mei, of me, tui, of thee, sui, of himself, nostri, of us, vestri, of you, (the genitive cases of their primitives ego, tu, &c.) are used when a person is signified, as

Languet desiderio tui:
He languishes for want of you.

You cannot give a more acceptable piece of information than the above, to any young lady. The fairer and more amiable sex always like to have something—if not to love, at least to pity.

Parsque tui lateat corpore clausa meo. —*Eton Gram.*
And a part of you may lie shut up in my body.

Or rather *may* it so lie! How forcibly a sucking pig hanging up outside a pork-butcher's shop always recals this beautiful line of Ovid's to the mind!

Meus, mine, tuus, thine, suus, his own (Cocknicè his'n), noster, ours, vester, yours, are used when action, or the possession of a thing is signified; as

Qui bona quæ non sunt sua furtim subripit, ille
Tempore quo capitur, carcere clausus erit:

Him as prigs wot isn 't his'n,
Ven he's cotch'd 'll go to pris'n.

These possessive pronouns, meus, tuus, suus, noster, and vester, take after them these genitive cases,—ipsius, of himself, solius, of him alone, unius, of one, duorum, of two, trium, of three, &c., omnium, of all, plurium, of more, paucorum, of few, cujusque, of every one, and also the genitive cases of participles, which are referred to the primitive word understood; as

> Meis unius impensis pocula sex exhausi:
> I drank six pots to my own cheek.

We wonder that any one should have the *face* to say so.

Sui and suus are reciprocal pronouns, that is, they have always relation to that which went before, and was most to be noted in the sentence, as—

> Jonathanus nimium admiratur se:
> Jonathan admires himself too much.
> Parcit erroribus suis, He spares his own errors.
> Magnoperè Jonathanus rogat ne se derideas, Jonathan earnestly begs that
>   you would not laugh at him.

If you *do*, take care that he does not *blow you up* one of these fine days.

These demonstrative pronouns, hic, iste, and ille are thus distinguished: hic points out the nearest to me; iste him who is by you; ille him who is at a distance from both of us.

In making *game* of the Syntax, we regard them as *pointers*.

When hic and ille are referred to two things or persons going before, hic generally relates to the latter, ille to the former, as

> Richardus Thomasque suum de more bibebant,
> Ebrius hic vappis, ebrius ille mero:
> Both Dick and Tom caroused away like swine,
> Tom drunk with swipes, and Dicky drunk with wine.

THE CONSTRUCTION OF VERBS.
THE NOMINATIVE CASE AFTER THE VERB.

Verbs substantive, as sum, I am, forem, I might be, fio, I am made, existo, I am; verbs passive of calling, as nominor, I am named, appellor, I am called, dicor, I am said, vocor, I am called, nuncupor, I am named, and the like to them, as videor, I am seen, habeor, I am accounted, existimor, I am thought, have the same cases before and after them, as

> Adeps viridis est summum bonum:
> Green fat is the chief good.

Even among the ancients, *turtles* were the emblems of love; which, next to eating and drinking, has always been the first object of human pursuit. This fact proves, very satisfactorily, two things, first, their proficiency in the science of gastronomy; and, secondly, their extreme susceptibility of the tender passion.

> Pileus vocatur tegula:

A hat is called a tile.

TILED IN.

Likewise all verbs in a manner admit after them an adjective, which agrees with the nominative case of the verb, in case, gender, and number, as

Pii orant taciti. —*Eton Gram.*
The pious pray silently.

Is this a sly rap at the Quakers?

The Genitive Case after the Verb.

Sum requires a genitive case as often as it signifies possession, duty, sign, or that which relates to any thing; as

Quod rapidam trahit Ætatem pecus est Melibœi,
The cattle *wot* drags the *Age*, fast coach, is Melibœus's.

Alas! that such an Age should be banished by the Age of rail-roads!—let us hear the

Coachman's Lament.

Air.—"Oh give me but my Arab steed."

Farewell my ribbons, and, alack!
Farewell my tidy drag;
Mail-coach-men now have got the *sack,*

And engineers the *bag*.

My heart and whip alike are broke—
I've lost my varmint team
That used to cut away like *smoke*,
But could n't go like *steam*.

It is, indeed, a bitter *cup*,
Thus to be sent to *pot*;
My bosom boils at boiling up
A gallop or a trot.

My very brain with *fury*'s rack'd,
That railways are the *rage*;
I'm sure you'll never find them *act*,
Like our old English *stage*.

A man whose *passion*'s crost, is sore,
Then pray excuse my *pet*;
I ne'er was *overturn'd* before,
But now am quite *upset*.

These nominative cases are excepted from the above rule, meum, mine, tuum, thine, suum, his, noster, our, vester, your, humanum, human, belluinum brutal, and the like, as

>Non est tuum aviam instruere:
>Don't teach your grandmother—to suck eggs.
>Humanum est inebriari.
>It is a human frailty—or an amiable weakness—to get drunk.

Lord Byron proves it to be a *human* frailty.

>"*Man* being *reasonable, must* get drunk."

A REASONABLE CREATURE.

Another poet (anon.) proves it to be an *amiable* one, by establishing the analogy which exists between it and an intoxication of another kind—

>"Love is like a dizziness,
>Never lets a poor man go about his business."

Verbs of accusing, condemning, advising, acquitting, and the like, require a genitive case which signifies the charge; as

>Qui alterum accusat probri, eum ipsum se intueri oportet.
>It is fit that he who accuses another of dishonesty should look into himself.

If this maxim were acted up to, what attorney could we ever get to frame an indictment?

>Furti damnatus, "tres menses" adeptus est:
>Being condemned of theft, he had "three months."

We do not see much *fun* in that. We cannot help thinking, however, that "Three Months at Brixton," would form a taking (at least a *thief*-taking) title for a novel.

>Admoneto magistrum squalidarum vestium:
>Put the master in mind of his seedy clothes.

That is if you want a *good dressing*.

This genitive case is sometimes changed into an ablative, either with or without a preposition, as

> Putavi de calendis Aprilibus te esse admonendum:
> I thought that you ought to be reminded of the first of April.

Young reader! were you ever, on the above anniversary, sent to the cobbler's for pi-geons' milk, and dismissed with *strap-oil* for your *pains*? Were your domestic and alimentive affections ever sported with by the false intelligence that a letter from home and a large cake were waiting for you below! Or worse, did some waggish, but inconsiderate friend ever send you a fool's-cap and a hamper of stones?

Reader, of a more advanced age, were you ever?— but we cannot go on—Oh! Matilda—we might have been your *slave*—but it was cruel of you to *sell* us in such a manner.

Uterque, both, nullus, none, alter, the other, neuter, neither of the two, alius, another, ambo, both, and the superlative degree, are joined to verbs of that kind only in the ablative case, as

> Fratris, an asini, trucidationis accusas me? Utroque, sed sceleris unius:
> Do you accuse me of killing my brother or my donkey? Of both; but of
>   one crime.

Satago, to be busy about a thing, misereor and miseresco, to pity, require a genitive case, as

> Qui ducit uxorem rerum satagit:
> He who marries a wife has his hands full of business.

We hear frequently of lovers being *distracted*. Husbands are much more so.

> O! tergi miserere mei non digna ferentis:
> Oh! have pity on my back, suffering things undeserved.

Reminiscor, to remember, obliviscor, to forget, memini, to remember, record-er, to call to mind, admit a genitive or accusative case, as

> Reminiscere nonarum Novembrium:
> Remember the fifth of November.

No wonder that so many *squibs* are let off on that day; considering the political feeling connected with it.

> Hoc te spectantem me meminisse precor:
> When this you see remember me.

How particularly anxious all young men and women who are lovers, and all waiters and chambermaids, whether they are lovers or no, besides coachmen and porters of all kinds, seem to be *remembered*. A coachman in one respect especially resembles a lover; he always wishes to be remembered by his *fare*.

Potior, to gain, is joined either to a genitive or to an ablative case, as

> Xantippe, marito subacto, femoralium potita fuit.
> Xantippe, her husband being overcome, gained the breeches.
> Terentius Thrace potitus est:

Terence got a Tartar.

At least he said he did, when he took the prisoner who would n't let him come.

The Dative Case after the Verb.

All verbs govern a dative case of that thing to or for which any thing is gotten or taken away, as

> Diminuam tibi caput:
> I will break your head.
> Eheu! mihi circulum ademit!
> Oh dear, he has taken away my hoop!

What a thing it is to be a junior boy!

Verbs of various kinds belong to the above rule. In the first place verbs signifying advantage or disadvantage govern a dative case, as

> Judæi ad commodandum nobis vivunt:
> The Jews live to accommodate us.

Or accommodate us to live—which?

Of these juvo, lædo, delecto, and some others, require an accusative case, as

> Maritum quies plurimum juvat:
> Rest very much delighteth a married man—when he can get it.

Verbs of comparing govern a dative case, as

> Ajacem "Surdo" componere sæpe solebam:
> I was often accustomed to compare Ajax to the "Deaf un,"—not because

he was hard of hearing, but hard in hitting.

Sometimes, however, they require an ablative case with the preposition cum; sometimes an accusative case with the prepositions ad and inter, as

Comparo *Pompeium* cum *globo nivali*:
I compare *Pompey* with a *snow-ball*.

Pompey is called in the schools a proper name. Whether it is a *proper name* for a nigger or not, may be questioned. It may also be doubted whether a negro can ever rightly be called "snow-ball," except he be *an ice* man; in which case even though he should be the knave of *clubs*, it is obvious that he ought never to be *black balled*.

Si ad pensum verberatio comparetur nihil est:
If a flogging be compared to an imposition, it is nothing.

A flogging is a fly-blow, or at least a *flea*-blow to the boy, and a task only to the master; whereas an imposition is a task to the boy, and very often a *verse* task.

Verbs of giving and of restoring govern a dative case, as

Learius unicuique filiarum dimidium coronæ dedit:
Lear gave his daughters half-a-crown a-piece.

Hence we are enabled to gain some notion of the great value of money in the time of the Ancient Britons.

Verbs of promising and of paying govern a dative case; as

Menelaus Paridi fustuarium promisit:
Menelaus promised Paris a drubbing.

"Gubernatoris" est pendere sartoribus pecuniam:
It is the place of "the governor" to pay tailors.

Hence young men may learn how desirable it is to be "in statu pupillari." True, in that state of felicity, they are somewhat under control, but the above example, and many others of a like nature, sufficiently prove, that such restriction, compared to the responsibilities of manhood, is but a *minor* inconvenience.

Verbs of commanding and telling govern a dative case, as

Alexander, vinosus, animis imperare non potuit:
Alexander, when drunk, could not command his temper.

Thus, in a state of beer, he committed manslaughter at least, by killing and slaying his friend Clitus. We could not resist the temptation to mention this fact, since, as we have so often laughed at its narration in those interesting compositions called themes, we thought there must needs be something very funny about it. Alexander the Great, be it remarked, for the special behoof of schoolboys, furnishes an example of any virtue or vice descanted on in any prose task or poem under the sun.

Antonio dixit Augustus Lepidum veteratorem fuisse.
Augustus told Antony that Lepidus was a humbug.

We don't know exactly where this historical fact is mentioned. *Lepidus* is a *funny* name.

Except, from the foregoing rule, rego, to rule, guberno, to govern, which have an accusative case; tempero and moderor, to rule, which have sometimes a dative, sometimes an accusative case; as

Luna regit ministros:
The moon rules the ministers.

That is to say, when it is at the full, and resembles a great O.

Præco pauperes gubernat:
The beadle governs the paupers.

Non semper temperat ipse sibi:
He does not always govern himself.

Non animos mollit proprios, nec temperat iras:
He neither softens his own mind, nor tempers his anger.

Ecce, Ducrow moderatur equos:
Lo, Ducrow manages the horses.

Q. Why is a general officer like a writing-master?

A. Because he is a *ruler of lines.*

Verbs of trusting govern a dative case, as

Credite, fœmineæ, juvenes, committere menti,
Nil nisi lene decet.
Believe me, young men, it is fit to entrust nothing to a female mind but

what is *soft*.

In fact, *soft nothings* are fittest for the ear of a lady.

Pomarius poetæ non credit:
The costermonger trusts not the poet.

How wrong, therefore, it is to call him a *green* grocer.

Verbs of complying with and of opposing govern a dative case, as

Nunquam obtemperat tiro hodiernus magistro:
A modern apprentice never obeys his master.

Verbs of threatening and of being angry govern a dative case, as

Utrique latronum mortem est minitatus:
He threatened death to both of the robbers, —

By presenting a pistol right and left at each of them. This when done by some well-disposed sailor in a melodrame, constitutes a situation of thrilling interest.

Sum with its compounds, except possum, governs a dative case, as

Oculi nigri non semper sunt faciei ornamentum:
Black eyes are not always an ornament to the face.

Verbs compounded with these adverbs, bene, well, satis, enough, male, ill, and with these prepositions, præ, ad, con, sub, ante, post, ob, in, inter, for the most part govern a dative case, as

Saginatio multis hominibus benefacit:
Cramming does good to many men.

For instance, it does good to aldermen, especially in these days of reform, *by enlarging the Corporation*. Cramming, or rather the effect of it, benefits medical men, who again do good to their patients by *cramming* them in another way. There is also a species of cramming which is found very serviceable at the Universities, by enabling certain students to *pass in a crowd*.

OH! HERE 'S A COMPLIMENT.

In this respect however it differs essentially from aldermanic cramming, which enhances the difficulty of such a feat in a very remarkable manner.

> Puellæ, aliæ aliis prælucere student:
> Girls endeavour to outshine one another.

And yet they *make light*, as much as they can, of each other's charms and accomplishments.

> Intempestive parum longe prospicienti Doctori adlusit.
> He joked unseasonably on the short-sighted Doctor.

Johnson was not so short-sighted as to be blind to a joke.

Not a few of the verbs mentioned in the last rule, sometimes change the dative into another case; as

> Præstat ingenio alius alium:
> One exceeds another in ability.

Thus one boy learns Latin and Greek better than the rest; another learns slang. One is a good hand at construing, another at climbing. Some boys are peculiarly skilled at casting accounts, others in casting stones. Here we have a boy of a small appetite and many words, there one of a large appetite and few words. Sometimes precocious talent is evinced for playing the fiddle, sometimes for playing a *stick*; sometimes, again, a strong propensity is discovered for playing the fool. This boy makes verses, as it were, by inspiration; that boy shows an equal capacity in making mouths. The most peculiar talent, however, and the one most exclusive of all others, is that of riding. Those who are destined to attain great proficiency in this science, can seldom do any thing else; and usually begin their career by being *horsed* at school.

Est, for habeo to have, governs a dative case, as

> Est mihi qui vestes custodit avunculus omnes:
> I have an uncle who takes care of all my clothes.

Suppetit, it sufficeth, is like to this, as

> Pauper enim non est cui rerum suppetit usus:
> For he is not poor, to whom the use of things suffices.

The two last examples must suggest a rather alarming idea to those who are accustomed to propitiate the relation to whom we have just alluded, by relinquishing *their habits*. Is it possible that he can ever *use* one's *things*? We recommend this query to the serious consideration of theatrical persons, and all others who are addicted to *spouting*.

Sum with many *others* admits a double dative case, as

> Exitio est avidis alvus pueris:
> The belly is the destruction of greedy boys.

Particularly those of *Eton* College.

Sometimes this dative case tibi, or sibi, or also mihi, is added for the sake of elegance in expression, as

> Cato suam sibi uxorem Hortensio vendidit:
> Cato sold his own wife to Hortensius.

Some say he only lent her. The fact most probably is, that the lady, being tired of her husband, wished to be a-*loan*.

THE ACCUSATIVE CASE AFTER THE VERB.

Verbs transitive, of what kind soever, whether active, deponent, or common, require an accusative case, as

> Procuratorem fugito, nam subdolus idem est:
> Avoid an attorney, for the same is a cunning rogue.

Yet the legal profession are always boasting of their *deeds*.

Verbs neuter have an accusative case of a like signification to themselves, as

> Pomarii asinus duram servit servitutem:
> A coster-monger's donkey serves a hard servitude.

Poor animal! A *Sterne* heart was once melted by thy sufferings—how then must they affect that of the *gentle* reader?

There are some verbs which have an accusative case by a figure, as

> Nec vox hominem sonat;
> Nor does your voice sound like a human creature's.

This may be said of boys of various kinds—as pot-boys, butcher's boys, baker's boys, and other boys who are in the habit of bawling down areas; also of several descriptions of men, as cab-men, coach-men, watch-men, and dust-men. The same may likewise be asserted of some women, such as apple-women, oyster-women, fish-women, and match-women. Here also the singing of charity children of both sexes, and the voices of parish-clerks, may be specified, and, lastly, of many foreigners whose names terminate in ini.

Verbs of asking, of teaching, of clothing, and of concealing, commonly govern two accusative cases, as

> Ego docebo te, adolescentule, lectiones tuas:
> *I'll* teach you your lessons, young man.

This speech is usually the prelude to something which elicits that exemplification of the vocative case which has been given in the first part of the Grammar.

Some verbs of this kind have an accusative case even in the passive voice, as

> Bis denos posceris versus de scoparum manubrio:

You are required to make twenty verses on a broomstick.

Why should not a broomstick form the subject of a poetical effusion, when the material of the broom itself is so often used in schools to stimulate inventive genius?

Nouns appellative are commonly added with a preposition to verbs which denote motion, as

> Interea ad templum non æquæ Palladis ibant Crinibus Iliades passis.
> *Virgil.*
> In the mean time the Trojan woman went to the temple of unfriendly Pallas with their hair about their ears.

How odd they must have looked. Here we take occasion to remind schoolboys never to lose an opportunity of giving a comic rendering to any word or phrase susceptible thereof, which they may meet with in the course of their reading. To say "crinibus passis", — "with dishevelled hair" would be to give a very feeble and spiritless translation. Vir is literally construed *man*; some school-masters will have it called *hero*, — we propose to translate it *cove*. So dapes may be rendered *grub*, or perhaps *prog*; aspera Juno, *crusty Juno*; animam efflare, to *kick the bucket*; capere fugam, to *cut one's stick*, or *lucky*; confectus, *knocked up*; fraudatus, *choused*; contundere, *to whop*, &c. &c.

THE ABLATIVE CASE AFTER THE VERB.

Every verb admits an ablative case, signifying the instrument, or the cause, or the manner of an action, as

> Pulvere nitrato Catilina senatum subruere voluit:
> Catiline wished to blow up the Parliament. Catiline was a regular Guy.

A noun of price is put after some words in the ablative case, as

> Ovidius solidis duobus fibulas siphonem ascendere fecit:
> Ovid pawned his buckles for two shillings.

The *sipho* was a tube, pipe, or spout, projecting from the shops of pawnbrokers, of whom there is every reason to believe that there were a great many in ancient Rome. Into this *sipho* the pledges were placed in order to be conveyed to the *adytum* or secret recess of the dwelling. *Vide* Casaubon de Avunc: Roman.

Vili, at a low rate, paulo, for little, minimo, for very little, magno, for much, nimio, for too much, plurimo, for very much, dimidio, for half, duplo, for twice as much, are often put by themselves, the word, pretio, price, being understood, as

> Vili venit cibus caninus:
> Dog's meat is sold at a low rate.

These genitive cases put without substantives are excepted, tanti, for so much, quanti, for how much, pluris, for more, minoris, for less, quantivis, for as much as you please, tantidem, for just so much, quantilibet, for what you will, quanticunque for how much soever, as

> Non es tanti: You're no great shakes.

Flocci, of a lock of wool, nauci, of a nut-shell, nihili, of nothing, assis, of a penny, pili, of a hair, hujus, of this, teruncii, of a farthing, are added very properly to verbs of esteeming, as

> Nec verberationem flocci pendo, nec ferulâ percussionem pili æstimo:
> I don't value a flogging a straw, nor do I regard a spatting a hair.

A boy who can say this, must have a brazen front, and an iron back, and be altogether a lad of *mettle*.

Verbs of abounding, of filling, of loading, and their contraries, are joined to an ablative case, as

> Tauris abundat Hibernia:
> Ireland aboundeth in bulls.

This circumstance it most probably was which gave rise to the *Tales* of the O'Hara family.

We once heard a son of Erin, while undergoing the operation of bleeding from the arm, remark that that would be an easy way of *cutting one's throat*.

Some of these sometimes govern a genitive case, as

> Optime ostrearum implebantur:
> They had a capital blow out of oysters.

We are sorry to remark that these are the only *native* productions patronized by great people.

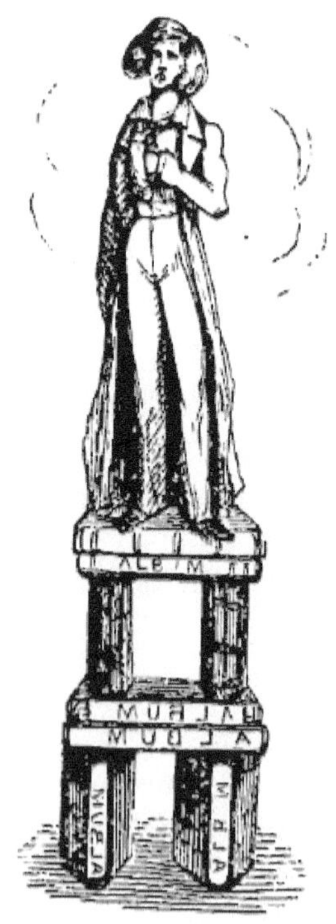

Fungor, to discharge, fruor, to enjoy, utor, to use, vescor, to live upon, dignor, to think one's self worthy, muto, to change, communico, to communicate, super-sedeo, to pass by, are joined to an ablative case, as

> Qui adipisci cœnas optimas volet, leonis fungatur officiis.
> He who shall desire to obtain excellent dinners, should discharge the
>   office of a lion.

In which case he will come in for the "lion's share."

Q. Why is the lion of a party like one of the grand sources of prejudice mentioned by Lord Bacon?

A. Because he is the *Idol* of the *den*.

Mereor, to deserve, with these adverbs, bene, well, satis, enough, male, ill, melius, better, pejus, worse, optime, very well, pessime, very ill, is joined to an ablative case with the preposition de, as

> De libitinario medicus bene meretur:
> The doctor deserves well of the undertaker.

Notwithstanding it might at first sight appear, that the doctor, in *furnishing funerals*, invades the undertaker's province.

Some verbs of receiving, of being distant, and of taking away, are sometimes joined to a dative case, as

> Augustus eripuit mihi nitorem:
> Augustus has taken the shine out of me.

> *Last Dying Speech of M. Antony.*

An ablative case, taken absolutely, is added to some verbs, as

> Porcis volentibus lætissime epulabimur:
> Please the pigs we'll have a jolly good dinner.

The pig had divine honours paid to it by the ancient Greeks. —Jos. Scalig. de Myst. Eleusin.

An ablative case of the part affected, and by the poets an accusative case, is added to some verbs, as

> Qui animo ægrotat, eum aera risum moventem ducere oportet.
> He who is sick in mind should breathe the laughing gas.

Much learned controversy has been expended in endeavouring to determine whether this gas was the exhalation by which it is supposed that the ancient Pythonesses were affected.

> Rubet nasum: Candet genas:
> His nose is red.   His cheeks are pale.

Some of these words are used also with the genitive case, as

> Angitur animi juvenis iste, et mundum indignatur.
> That young man is grieved in mind and disgusted with the world.

Such a man is called by the ladies an interesting young man.

Verbs Passive.

An ablative case of the doer (but with the preposition a or ab going before), and sometimes also a dative case, is added to verbs passive, as

> Darius eleganter ab Alexandro victus est:
> Darius was elegantly licked by Alexander.

The other cases continue to belong to verbs passive which belonged to them as verbs active, as

> Titanes læsæ majestatis accusati sunt:
> The Titans were indicted for high treason.

And being found guilty were *quartered* in a very uncomfortable manner, as well as *drawn* by various artists, whose skill in *execution* has been much commended.

Vapulo, to be beaten, veneo, to be sold, liceo, to be prized, exulo, to be banished, fio, to be made, neuter passives, have a passive construction, as

> A præceptore vapulabis. *Eton Gram.*
> You will be beaten by the master.

It appears to us that vapulo, to be beaten, is here at all events more susceptible of a passive construction than a funny one.

> Malo a cive spoliari quam ab hoste venire. *Eton Gram.*
> I had rather be stripped by a citizen than sold by an enemy.

The Romans were regularly *sold* by the enemy for once, when they had to go under the yoke.

Verbs of the Infinitive Mood.

Verbs of the infinitive mood are put after some verbs, participles, and adjectives, and substantives also by the poets, as

> Timotheus ursos saltare fecit:
> Timotheus made the bears dance.

This was done in ancient as it is in modern times, by playing the Pandean pipes.

> Inconcinnus erat cerni Telamonius Ajax;
> Ajax (ut referunt) vir bonus ire minor:

> The Telamonian Ajax was a rum un to look at;
> The lesser Ajax (as they say) a good un to go.

The Grecians used to call Ajax senior, the *fighting cock,* and Ajax junior, the *running cock.*

Verbs of the infinitive mood are sometimes placed alone by the figure ellipsis, as

> Siphonum de more oculis demittere fluctus Dardanidæ:

The Trojans (began understood) to pipe their eyes.

As for Æneas he might have been a town *crier*.

Gerunds and Supines.

govern the cases of their own verbs, as

Efferor studio pulices industrios videndi:
I am transported with the desire of seeing the industrious fleas.

Gerunds.

"When Dido found Æneas would not come,
She mourned in silence, and was Di-do-dum."

Gerunds in di have the same construction as genitive cases, and depend both on certain substantives and adjectives, as

Londinensem innatus amor civem urget edendi:
An innate love of eating excites the London citizen.

People are accustomed to utter a great deal of cant about the intellectual poverty of civic magistrates, and common councilmen in general; but it must be allowed that those respectable individuals have often *a great deal in them*.

TURTUR ALDERMANICUS.

Gerunds in do have the same construction with ablative, and gerunds in dum with accusative cases, as

> Scribendi ratio conjuncta cum loquendo est:
> The means of writing are joined with speaking.

Some things are written precisely after the writer's way of speaking. We once, for example, saw the following notice posted in a gentleman's preserve.

> Whear 'as Gins and Engens are Set on Thes Grouns for the Destruction Of Varmint, Any trespussing Will be prossy-Cuted a-cordin Too Law.

> Locus ad agendum amplissimus:
> A place very honourable to plead in.

It may be questioned whether Cicero would have said this of the Old Bailey.

When necessity is signified, the gerund in dum is used without a preposition, the verb est being added.

> Cavendum est ne deprênsus sis:
> You must take care you 're not caught out.

A piece of advice of special importance to schoolboys on many occasions, such as the following: shirking down town; making devils, or letting off gunpowder behind the school, or in the yard; conducting a foray or predatory excursion in gardens and orchards; emulating Jupiter, à la Salmoneus,—in his attribute of Cloud-Compelling—by blowing a cloud, or to speak in the vernacular, indulging in a cigar; hoisting a frog; tailing a dog or cat, or in any other way acting contrary to the precepts of the Animals' Friend Society; learning to construe on the Hamiltonian system; furtively denuding the birch-rods of their "budding honours." Cum multis aliis quæ nunc perscribere longum est.

Gerunds are also changed into nouns adjective, as

Ad faciendos versus molestum est:
It is a bore to make verses.

This being a self-evident proposition, we shall not enlarge upon it.

The supine in um signifies actively, and follows a verb expressing motion to a place, as

Spectatum veniunt, veniunt spectentur ut ipsæ:
They come to see, they come that they themselves may be seen.

So said, or sung the poet Ovid. Was there an opera at Rome in his time?

The supine in u signifies passively, and follows nouns adjective, as

Quod olfactu fœdum est, idem est et esu turpe:

That which is foul to be smelled, is also nasty to be eaten.

Except venison, onions, and cheese.

Nouns of Time and Place.
Time.

Tempus—time. There is a story, mentioned (we quote from memory) by the learned Joe Miller; of a fellow who seeing "Tempus Fugit" inscribed upon a clock, took it for the name of the artificer.

Persons who have lived a long *time* in the world, are generally accounted *sage*; and are sometimes considered to have had a good *seasoning*.

Nouns which signify a part of time are put more commonly in the ablative case, as

> Nemo mortalium omnibus horis sapit:
> No mortal man is wise at all hours.

The excuse of a philosopher for getting married.

But nouns which signify the duration of time are commonly put in the accusative case, as

> Pugna inter juvenem Curtium et Titum Sabinum tres horas perduravit.
> The fight between young Curtius and Sabine Titus lasted three hours.

It is an error to suppose that Roman mills were only water-mills and wind-mills. The above mill must have been rather a "winder" though, and must have cost the combatants much *pains*.

We say also: in paucis diebus, in a few days: de die, by day, de nocte, by night, &c.

A jest upon the nouns of *Time* would, perhaps, be somewhat ill timed: we hope, however, to have *Space* for one presently.

The Space of a Place.

The space of a place is put in the accusative, and sometimes also in the ablative, as

> Cæsar jam mille passus processerat, summâ diligentiâ.
> Cæsar had now advanced a mile with the greatest diligence—not on the
>   top of the vehicle so named, as a young gentleman was once flogged
>   for saying.
> Qui non abest a scholâ centenis millibus passuum, balatronem novi.
> I know a blackguard who is not absent a hundred miles from the school.

"Cantare et apponere" to sing and apply, is the maxim we would here inculcate on our youthful readers.

Every verb admits a genitive case of the name of a city or town in which any thing takes place, so that it be of the first or second declension, and of the singular number, as

> Quid Romæ faciam? mentiri nescio:
> What shall I do at Rome? I know not how to lie.

What a bare-faced perversion of the truth that cock and bull story is of Curtius jumping into the hole in the forum. How the Romans managed to get *credit* from any body but the tailors is to us a mystery.

These genitive cases, humi, on the ground, domi, at home, militiæ, in war, belli, in war, follow the construction of proper names, as

> Parvi sunt foris arma nisi est consilium domi:
> Arms are of little worth abroad unless there be wisdom at home.

Cicero must have said this with a prospective eye to Canada.

But if the name of a city or town shall be of the plural number only, or of the third declension, it is put in the ablative case, as

> Aiunt centum portas Thebis fuisse:
> They say there were an hundred gates at Thebes.

You needn't believe it unless you like.

> Egregia Tibure facta videnda sunt:
> Fine doings are to be seen at Tivoli.

The name of a place is often put after verbs signifying motion to a place in the accusative case without a preposition, as

> Concessi Cantabrigiam ad capiendum ingenii cultum:
> I went to Cambridge to become a fast man.

After this manner we use domus, a house, and rus, the country, as Rus ire jussus sum, I was rusticated. Domum missus eram, I was sent home.

Going *too fast* at Cambridge sometimes necessitates, in two senses, a dose of country air.

The name of a place is sometimes added to verbs signifying motion from a place, in the ablative case without a proposition, as

> Arbitror te Virginiâ veteri venisse:
> I reckon you've come from old Virginny.

VERBS IMPERSONAL.

Verbs impersonal have no nominative case, as

> Scenas post tragicas multum juvat ire sub umbras:
> After a tragedy it is very pleasant to go under the *Shades*.

The worst of these "Shades" is, that people are now and then apt to get rather "too much in the sun" there.

These impersonals, interest, it concerns, and refert, it concerns, are joined to any genitive cases, except these ablative cases feminine, meâ, tuâ, suâ, nostrâ, vestrâ, and cujâ, as

> Interest magistratûs tueri insulsos, animadvertere in acres.
> It concerns the magistrate to defend the flats; to punish the sharps.

These genitive cases also, are added, tanti, of so much, quanti, of how much, magni, of much, parvi, of little, quanticunque, of how much soever, tantidem, of just so much; as

> Tanti refert honesta agere;
> Of such consequence is it to do honest things.

By this course of conduct, you certainly render yourself worthy of the protection of the magistrate; although whether you thereby constitute yourself a flat or not, is perhaps a doubtful question. Much may be said on both sides. Dishonesty, it is true, may lead to being taken up; but then honesty often leads to being taken *in*. Yet honesty is said to be the best policy. Policy is a branch of wisdom, and "wisdom" they say "is in the *wig*." Certain *wigs* are retained at the *head*—of affairs, by a good deal of *policy*; perhaps the *best* they could adopt—a fact that throws considerable doubt on the truth of the old maxim.

Impersonal verbs which are put acquisitively, require a dative case; but those which are put transitively an accusative, as—

> A ministris nobis benefit:
> We enjoy blessings from Ministers.

For instance—No—We cannot think of any just at present.

> Me juvat per lunam errare, et "Isabellam" cantare:
> I like to wander by moonlight, and sing "Isabelle."

The connexion between love and moonlight is as interesting as it is certain. We shrewdly suspect that the said planet has more to do with the tender passion than lovers are aware of.

But the preposition *ad* is peculiarly *ad*ded to these verbs—attinet, it belongs, pertinet, it pertains, spectat, it concerns, as

> Spectat ad omnes bene vivere:
> It concerns all to live well—

When they can afford it.

An accusative case with a genitive is put after these verbs impersonal—pœnitet, it repents, tædet, it wearies, miseret, miserescit, it pities, pudet, it shames, piget, it grieves, as—

> "Nihil me pœnitet hujus nasi"—Trist: Shand:
> "My nose has been the making of me."

A verb impersonal of the passive voice may be elegantly taken for each person of both numbers; that is to say, by virtue of a case added to it.

Thus statur is used for sto, stas, stat, stamus, statis, stant. Statur a me; it is stood by me, that is, I stand; statur ab illis: it is stood by them, or they stand.

King George the Fourth's statue at King's Cross is a *standing joke*.

THE CONSTRUCTION OF PARTICIPLES.

Participles govern the cases of the verbs from which they are derived, as—

> Duplices tendens ad sidera palmas, Talia voce refert:
> Stretching forth his hands to heaven, he utters *such* things.

This reminds us of the Italian opera.

A dative case is sometimes added to participles of the passive voice, especially when they end in dus, as—

> Sollicito nasus rutilans metuendus amanti est:
> A fiery nose is to be feared by an anxious lover.

Participles, when they become nouns, require a genitive case, as—

> Vectigalis appetens, linguæ profusus:
> Greedy of *rint*, lavish of blarney.

Exosus, hating, perosus, utterly hating, pertæsus, weary of, signifying actively, require an accusative case, as—

> Philosophus exosus ad unam mulieres:
> A philosopher hating women in general, *i.e.* a Malthusian.

Exosus, hated, and perosus, hated to death, signifying passively, are read with a dative case, as

> Comœdi sanctis exosi sunt:
> The comedians are hated by the saints.

We mean the spiritual Quixotes, or Knights of the Rueful Countenance. We "calculate" that they will be the greatest patrons of rail roads, considering their dislike to the *stage*.

Natus, born, prognatus, born, satus, sprung, cretus, descended, creatus, produced, ortus, risen, editus, brought forth, require an ablative case, and often with a preposition, as—

> Taffius, bonis prognatus parentibus, cerevisiam haud tenuem de sese existimat:
> Taffy, sprung of good parents, thinks no small beer of himself.
> De Britannis Antiquis se jactat editum:
> He boasts of being descended from the Ancient Britons.

Q. Why is the eldest son of a King of England like a Leviathan?

A. Because he is the Prince of *Wales*.

THE CONSTRUCTION OF ADVERBS.

En and ecce, adverbs of showing, are joined most commonly to a nominative case, to an accusative case but seldom, as

> En Romanus: See the Roman (q. rum-un.)
> Ecce Corinthium: Behold the Corinthian.

Modern Corinthians, we fear, know but little Greek, except that of the Ægidiac, or St. Giles's dialect.

En and ecce, adverbs of upbraiding, are joined most commonly to an accusative case only, as—

> En togam squamosam!
> Look at his scaly toga!
> Ecce caudam! Twig his tail!

Certain adverbs of time, place, and quantity, admit a genitive case, as

Ubi gentium est Quadra Russelliana?
Where in the world is Russell Square?

We must confess that this question is *exquisitely* absurd.

Nihil tunc temporis amplius quam flere poteram:
I could do nothing more at that time than weep.

Talking of weeping—how odd it is that an affectionate wife should cry when her husband is *transported* for life.

DOMESTIC ORATORY (SMALL BOY SPOUTING IN A CHAIR).

Domestic Elocution "My name is Norval on the Grampian Hills"

Satis eloquentiæ, sapientiæ parum:
Eloquence enough, wisdom little enough.

This quotation applies very forcibly to domestic oratory as practised by small boys at the instigation of their mamma, for the *amusement* of visitors. Those on whom "little bird with boothom wed," "deep *in* the windingths *of* a whale," or "my name is Nawval," and the like recitations are inflicted, have "satis eloquentiæ" — enough of eloquence, in all conscience; and we cannot but think that "sapientiæ parum," "wisdom little enough" is displayed by all the other parties concerned.

Some adverbs admit the cases of the nouns from which they are derived, as

Juvenis benevolus sibi inutiliter vivit:
The good-natured young man lives unprofitably to himself —

Especially if he have a large circle of female acquaintance.

These adverbs of diversity, aliter, otherwise, and secus, otherwise; and these two, ante, before, and post, after, are often joined to an ablative case, as —

Plure aliter. More t'other.

Multo ante. Much before.

Paulo post. Little behind.

Those who are much *before*, are guilty of a great *waste* — of time; and those who are little behind should make it up by a *bustle*.

Instar, like or equal to, and ergo, for the sake of, being taken as adverbs, have a genitive case after them, as —

Instar montis equum divina Palladis arte
Ædificant:
By the divine assistance of Pallas they build a horse as big as a mountain.

This may appear incredible; yet the learned Munchausenius relates prodigies much more astonishing.

> Mentitur Virgilius leporis ergo:
> Virgil tells lies for fun.

As may be sufficiently seen in the example before the last, and also in the sixth book of the Æneid, passim.

THE CONSTRUCTION OF CONJUNCTIONS.

Conjunctions copulative and disjunctive, couple like cases, moods, and tenses, as

> Socrates docuit Xenophontem et Platonem geographiam, astronomiam, et rationem globorum:
> Socrates taught Xenophon and Plato geography, astronomy, and the use of the globes.

Q. How may a waterman answer the polite interrogation "Who are you?" correctly, and designate at the same time, an educational institution.

A. By saying A-cad-am-I.

The foregoing rule (not riddle) holds good, unless the reason of a different construction requires it should be otherwise, as

> Emi librum centussi et pluris:
> I bought a book for a hundred pence, and more,

> "100*d.* are 8*s.* 4*d.*" —Walkinghame.

The conjunction, quam, than, is often understood after amplius, more, plus, more, and minus, less, as

> Amplius sunt sex menses:
> There are more than six months.

For this interesting piece of information we are indebted to Cicero. The author to whom reference has just been made, has somewhere, if we mistake not, a similar observation. In thus *ushering* the *Tutor's* Assistant into notice, we feel that we are citing a work of which it is impossible to make too comical mention.

Thank goodness there are not more than six months in a half year!

TO WHAT MOODS OF VERBS CERTAIN ADVERBS
AND CONJUNCTIONS DO AGREE.

Ne, an, num, whether put doubtfully or indefinitely, are joined to a subjunctive mood, as—

> Nihil refert fecerisne an persuaseris:
> It matters nothing whether you have done it or persuaded to it—

as the school-master said when he got hold of the wrong end of the cane.

Here it may be remarked—First, that the young gentlemen who play tricks with *tallow* are likely to get more *whacks* than they like on their fingers. Secondly—That a master whose hand is in *Grease* cannot be expected to be at the same time in *A-merry-key*.

Dum, for dummodo, so that, and quousque, until, requires a subjunctive mood, as—

Dum felix sis, quid refert?
What's the odds, so long as you're happy.

Qui, signifying the cause, requires a subjunctive mood, as

Stultus es qui Ovidio credas:
You are a fool for believing Ovid.

Ut, for, postquam, after that, sicut, as, and quomodo, how, is joined to an indicative mood; but when it signifies quanquam, although, utpote, forasmuch as, or the final cause, to a subjunctive mood, as

Ut sumus in Ponto ter frigore constitit Ister:
Since that we are in Pontus the Danube has stood frozen three times.

Were skating and sliding classical accomplishments? Ambition, we know, led many of the Romans to tread on *slippery* ground: many of them struck out new paths, but none (that we have heard of) ever struck out a slide. Imagine Cato or Seneca "coming the cobbler's knock."

Te oro, domine, ut exeam:
Please, sir, let me go out.

Lastly, all words put indefinitely, such as are these, quis, who, quantus, how great, quotus, how many, require a subjunctive mood, as

Cave cui incurras, inepte:
Mind who you run against, stupid.

Such may have been the speech of a Roman cabman. A very curious specimen of the *tessera*, or badge, worn on the breast by this description of persons, has lately been discovered at Herculaneum.

THE CONSTRUCTION OF PREPOSITIONS.

A preposition being understood, sometimes causes an ablative case to be added, as

> Habeo pigneratorem loco avunculi; *i.e.* in loco:
> I esteem a pawnbroker in the place of an uncle: that is, *in loco*.

A preposition in composition sometimes governs the same case which it also governed out of composition, as

> Jupiter Olympo Vulcanum calce exegit:
> Jupiter kicked Vulcan out of Olympus.

This was not only an ungentlemanly, but also an *ungodly* act on Jupiter's part. Reasoning à posteriori, one would think it must have been very unpleasant to Vulcan.

> Præteriit me in Quadrante insalutatum:
> He cut me in the Quadrant.

Verbs compounded with a, ab, de, e, ex, in, sometimes repeat the same prepositions with their case out of composition, and that elegantly, as

> Abstinuerunt a vino:
> They abstained from wine.

This properly is an allusion to the Tiber-totallers. It should be remembered that tea was unknown in Rome, except as the accusative case of a pronoun.

In, for, erga, towards, contra, against, ad, to, and supra, above, requires an accusative case, as

> Quietum
> Accipit in pueros animum mentemque benignam:
> He admits kind thoughts and inclinations towards the boys.

The master does—when he gives them a half holiday or a blow out. Mr. Squeers (vide Nicholas Nick: illustriss. Boz.) was in the habit of *making much* of the young gentlemen intrusted to his care.

Sub, when it relates to time, is commonly joined to an accusative case, as

> Sub idem tempus—Isaaculus trans maria deportatus est:
> About the same time—Ikey was transported beyond the seas.

We say *beyond the seas*, lest it should be questioned whether Mr. I. was *transported* as a necessary or contingent consequence of cheating.

Super, for, ultra, beyond, is put with an accusative case, for de, concerning, with an ablative case, as

> Super et Garamantas et Indos
> Proferet imperium:
> He will extend the empire both beyond the Africans and the Indians.

A wide *rule* expressed in poetical *measure*.

> Quid de domesticis Peruviorum rebus censeas?
> What may be your opinion concerning the domestic economy of the
> Peruvians?

Tenus, as far as, is joined to an ablative case, both in the singular and plural number, as

> Cervice, auribusque tenus Marius in luto inveniebatur:
> Marius was found up to his neck and ears in mud.

What a lark! or rather a mud lark. But tenus is joined to a genitive only in the plural, and it always follows its case, as

> Crurum tenus: up to the *legs*.

Which it is very necessary to be at Epsom and Ascot.

THE CONSTRUCTION OF INTERJECTIONS.

Interjections are often put without a case, as

> Spem gregis, ah! silice in nudâ connixa reliquit:
> Having yeaned, she left the hope of the flock, alas! upon the bare flint
> stones.

And exposed to the *steely*-hearted world, which, as an Irishman remarked, was a dangerous situation for *tinder* infancy. It must have been, to say the least, a most uncomfortable *berth*.

O! of one exclaiming, is joined to a nominative, accusative, and vocative case,
as

O lex! Oh law! O alaudas! Oh larks! Oh meum! Oh my! O care! Oh dear!

We cannot find out what is Latin for oh Crikey!

HEU! MISERANDE PUER! (BOY TOSSED IN A BLANKET)

Heu! and proh! alas! are joined, sometimes to a nominative, sometimes to an accusative, and occasionally to a vocative case, as—Heu bellis! Lack-a-*daisy*. Heu diem! Lack-a-*day*. Proh Clamor! Oh *cry*! Proh deos pisciculosque! Oh, ye gods and little fishes!

> Heu miserande puer!
> Oh, boy, to be pitied!

What boy is more to be pitied than a junior boy? The *Fagin* system described in Oliver Twist is nothing compared to that adopted in public schools. People may say what they will of the beneficial effect which it produces on the minds of those who are subjected to it—we contend that to breed a gentleman's son up like a *tiger* is the readiest way to make a *beast* of him.

Hei! and væ! alas, are joined to a dative case, as

> Hei mihi quod nullis amor est medicabilis herbis:
> Woe is me that love is curable by no herbs.

Ovid never would have said that, if he had smoked a cigar or chewed tobacco. The ancients believed that love might be excited by certain articles taken from the vegetable kingdom. Why then should it be considered impossible to allay the same feeling in a similar manner? Every bane has its corresponding antidote; if so, there may be physic even for a philter. And for the pangs which a *virgin* has inflicted, what remedy could be prescribed more reasonable than the *Virginian* weed;—besides, love generally ends in smoke.

A CURE FOR THE HEARTACHE.

Væ misero capiti, madefacto, sæpe fenestræ
Imbribus immundis, Lydia cara, tuæ:
Woe to my wretched head, often wetted, dear
Lydia, by the unclean showers of your window.

This would be a proper place for introducing a few remarks on the ancient mode of serenading; which we are prevented from doing by the very imperfect state of our present information on this interesting point. It is, however, pretty generally admitted that the Romans always took care to provide themselves with an umbrella on these occasions, and this for a reason which the above distich will have rendered sufficiently obvious. It appears to us that so salutary a precaution is well worthy of being sometimes adopted in these modern days—and with this hint we conclude the Syntax.

*   *   *   *   *

PROSODY.

All you that bards of note would be,
Must study well your Prosody.

As Comparative Anatomy teaches what the sound of a cod-fish is; so Prosody teaches what is the sound of syllables.

Sound and quantity mean the same thing; though how that fact is to be reconciled with the proverb, "great *cry* and little *wool*," we do not know.

Prosody is divided into three parts. Tone, Breathing, and Time. As to tone—boys are usually required to repeat it in a loud one, without stammering or drawling; and with as little breathing and time, or breathing-time, as possible.

We shall leave tone to the consideration of pianoforte and fiddle-makers; and breathing to doctors and chemists, who can *analyze* it a great deal better than we can. In this place we think proper to treat only of Time.

Now of Time a very great deal may be said, taking the word in all the senses in which it is capable of being used.

In the first place, Time flies—but this we have had occasion to observe before; as also that Time is a very great eater.

In the second, Time is a very ill-used personage; he is spent, wasted, lost, kicked down, and killed—the last as often as an Irishman is—but for all that he never complains.

It is a question whether keeping Time, or losing Time, is the essential characteristic of dancing.

Then we might expatiate largely about the value of Time, and of the propriety of taking him by the forelock—but for two reasons.

One of them is, that all this has been said long ago; the other, that it is nothing at all to the purpose.

We might also quote extensively from Dr. Culpeper's Herbal, and from Linnæus and Jussieu; but the *time* we speak of, (although we hope it will be *twigged* by the reader,) is no *plant*; nevertheless it is a necessary ingredient in grammatical *stuffing*.

Time in prosody is the measure of the pronouncing of a syllable.

Like whist, it is divided into Long and Short. A long time is marked thus, as sūmēns, taking: a short time thus; as pĭlŭlă, a pill.

A foot is the placing together of two or more syllables, according to the certain observation of their *time*, the organ of which should be well developed for that purpose.

Ordinary feet are long feet, short feet, broad feet, splay feet, club feet, and bumble feet, to which may be added cloven feet in the case of certain animals, and an "old gentleman."

There are several kinds of Latin feet; here, however, we shall only notice spondees and dactyls.

A spondee is a foot of two syllables, as īnfāns, an infant.

A dactyl is a foot of three syllables, as āngĕlŭs, an angel, pōrcŭlŭs, a little pig.

Scanning is measuring a verse as you are measured by your tailor—by the *foot*, according to *rule*. To scanning there belong the figures called Synalœpha, Ecthlipsis, Synæresis, Diæresis, and Cæsura.

Synalœpha is the cutting off a vowel at the end of a word, before another at the beginning of the next; as

> Ōcclūsīs ēvāsi ŏcŭlīs nāsōquĕ cruēntō:
> I came off with my eyes bunged up and a bloody nose.

We have here *knocked out an i* in evasi, on the strength of a synalœpha.

But heu and o are never cut off—at least there are no cases on record in which this operation has been performed.

Ecthlipsis is as often as the letter m is cut off with its vowel; the next word beginning with a vowel, as

> Mōnstrum hōrrēndum īnfōrme īngēns—spectāvĭmŭs hōrtīs:
> We saw a horrible, ugly, great monster in the gardens.

If every *bear* and *boar* were kept in a den—what a fine world this would be.

Synæresis is the contraction of two syllables into one, as in alvearia, pronounced alvaria.

> Strāvĭt hŭmī dēmēns cōnfērta ālveārĭă Jūnō:
> Mad Juno threw the crowded beehives on the ground.

Hydrophobia occurring in a queen bee from the bite of a dog would be an interesting case to the faculty.

Diæresis is the separation of one syllable into two, as evoluisse for evolvisse. Thus Ovid says, alluding probably to the *padding* system adopted by dandies and theatrical artists,

> Dēbŭĕrant fūsōs ēvŏlŭīssĕ sŭōs:
> They ought to have unwound their *spindles*.

Cæsura is when after a perfect foot (though not one like Taglioni's), a short syllable is made long at the end of a word, as

> Pēctŏrĭbūs ĭnhĭāns—mōllēs, ēn, dēsĕrĭt ālās:
> Intent upon the breasts (of the fowls) lo! he deserts the tender wings.

Of the Kinds of Verses.

Should any one seek here for an account of every kind of verse used by the Latin poets, all we can say is—we wish he may get it. As it behoveth no one to be wiser than the law, so it behoveth not us to be wiser than the Eton Grammar.

The verses which boys are commonly taught to make are hexameters and pentameters.

An hexameter verse consists of six feet. As the ancient heroes were at least six feet high, this is probably the reason why it is also called an *heroic* verse.

The fifth foot in this kind of verse should be a dactyl, the sixth a spondee; the other feet may be either dactyls or spondees; as

> Ōbstāntī plŭvĭīs vēnīt cūm tēgmĭnĕ Sāmbō:
> Sambo came with his Macintosh.

The fifth foot also is sometimes a spondee, as

> Clāvĭgĕr Ālcīdēs, māgnūm Jŏvĭs īncrēmēntūm.
> Hercules, king of clubs, great offspring of Jupiter.

The last syllable of every verse is a *common* affair.

An elegiac, lack-a-daisical, or pentameter verse, consists of four feet and two long syllables, one of which is placed between the second and third foot, and the other at the end of the verse. The two first feet may be dactyls, spondees, or both; the two last are always dactyls, as

> Rēs ēst īnfēlīx, plēnăquĕ frāudĭs ămōr:
> Love is an unlucky affair, and full of humbug.

We feel compelled, notwithstanding what has been before said, to make a few additions to what is contained in the Eton Grammar with respect to verses.

The rhythm of Latin verses may be easily learned by practising (out of school), exercises on the principle of the examples following—

> Dūm dĭdlĕ, dī dūm, dūm dūm, dēedlĕdy, dēēdlĕ dĕ, dūm dum;
> Dūm dĭdlĕ, dūm dum, dē, dēedlĕdy̆, dēedlĕdy̆, dūm.

N.B. The following familiar piece of poetry would not have been admitted into the Comic Latin Grammar, but that there being many various readings of it, we wished to transmit the right one to posterity.

> Patres conscripti—took a boat and went to Philippi.

Trumpeter unus erat qui coatum scarlet habebat,
Stormum surgebat, et boatum overset–ebat,
Omnes drownerunt, quia swimaway non potuerunt,
Excipe John Periwig tied up to the tail of a dead pig.

PATRES CONSCRIPTI TOOK A BOAT AND WENT TO PHILIPPI TRUM-
PETER UNUS ERAT QUI COATUM SCARLET HABEBAT.

Here, also, this poetical curiosity may perhaps be properly introduced.

Conturbabantur Constantinopolitani,
Innumerabilibus sollicitudinibus.

Of the Quantity of the first Syllable.

There is a river in Macedon and a river in Monmouth: in like manner there are positions in dancing and positions in Prosody.

The following vowels are long by position.

1. A vowel before two consonants, or before a double consonant in the same word—as pīnguis, fat, īngens, great, Ājax, the name of a hero.

2. A vowel coming before one consonant at the end of a word, and another at the beginning of the next, as

Majōr sūm quām cui possīt tua virga nocere:
I'm a bigger boy than your rod is able to hurt.

The syllables *jor*, *sum*, *quam*, and *sit*, are long by position.

3. Sometimes, but seldom, a short vowel at the end of a word placed before two consonants at the beginning of the next; as

Occultā spolia hi Croceo de Colle ferebant:
These persons brought the secret spoils from Saffron Hill.

A *short* vowel before a mute, a liquid following, is rendered common, as in the word *patris*.

Sunt quibus ornatur Jenkins femoralia pātris:
The breeches that Jenkins is rigged out in are his father's.

A vowel before another is always short, as tŭa, thy, memorĭa, memory.

Except the genitive cases of pronouns in ius, where the i is a common i, although alterĭus has always a short *i* and alīus a long *i*.

Except, likewise, those genitive and dative cases of the fifth declension where the vowel *e*, like Punch's nose, is made long between two *i*'s, as faciēi, of a face.

The syllable *fi* also in fīo is long, except e and r follow together, as fĭerem, fĭeri.

> Fĭent quæ "Fĭeri Facias" mandata vocantur:
> The writ which is called "Fieri Facias" will be made.

Fi. fa. is a legal instrument that deprives a poor man of his mattress that a rich one may lounge on his ottoman. Ca. Sa. is a similar benevolent contrivance for punishing misfortune as felony.

Dīus, heavenly, has the first syllable long;—Diana, common: and so has the interjection Ohe!

> Thus there's a common medium of connexion,
> Between a goddess and an interjection.

A vowel before another in Greek words is sometimes long, as

> Cærula, Pīerides, sunt vobis tegmina crurum:
> Oh, Muses, your stockings are blue.

Also in Greek possessives, as

> Somniculosa fuit, pinguisque Ænēia nutrix:
> Æneas's nurse was sleepy and fat.

Æneas has often enough been represented in *arms*.

> In Latin mark, that every dipthong
> 'S as long as any stage-coach whip-thong;
> Except before a vowel it goes,
> When 'tis as short as Elsler's clothes.

Words derived from others are tarred with the same stick, that is, are assigned the same quantity as those which they are derived from, with some few exceptions, which we must trouble the student to fish for.

Compounds follow the quantity of their simple words, as from lĕgo lĕgis, to read, comes perlĕgo, to read through.

By the way, *reading* does not always induce *reading through*; though we hope it may in the case of the C. L. G.

> If to a preterperfect tense belong
> Two only syllables, the first is long;
> As vēni, vīdi, vīci, speech so cool.
> Which Cæsar made to illustrate our rule;
> To which we need not cite exceptions small.
> Look in your Gradus and you'll find them all.

Consult also the Eton Grammar, and works of the poets, passim, as well for exceptions to the above as to the two following rules:

1. Words that double the first syllable of the preterperfect tense have the first syllable short—as cĕcĭdī from cădŏ, &c.

Fortis Higinbottom cĕcidit terramque mŏmordit:
Brave Higinbottom fell and bit the ground.

2. A supine of two syllables has the first syllable long—

As vīsum lātum lōtum mōtum:
And many more if we could quote 'em.

OF THE QUANTITY OF THE LAST SYLLABLE.

We have had a poetical fit gradually growing upon us for some time—'tis of no use
to resist—so here goes—

Oh! Muse, thine aid afford to me,
Inspire my Ideality;
Thou who, benign, in days of yore,
Didst heavenly inspiration pour
On him, who luckily for us
Sang Propria Quæ Maribus;
Teach me to sound on quiv'ring lyre,
Prosodial strains in notes of fire;
Words' ends shall be my theme sublime,
Now first descanted on in rhyme.

Come, little boys, attention lend,
All words are long in a that end:
(In proof of which I'll bet a quart,)
Excepting those which must be short—
As pută, ită, posteă, quiă,
Ejă, and every case in iă;
Or a, save such as we must class
With Grecian vocatives in as,
And ablatives of first declension—
Besides the aforesaid, we may mention
Nouns numeral that end in ginta,
Which common, as a bit of flint are.

Some terminate in *b, d, t;*
All these are short; but those in *c*
Form toes—I mean, form ends of feet
As long—as long as Oxford Street.
Though nĕc and donĕc every bard
Hath written short as Hanway yard,
Fac, hic, and hoc are common, though
Th' ablative hōc is long you know.

Now "*e* finita" short are reckon'd,
Like to a jiffey or a second,
Though we must call the *Gradus* wrong,
Or these, of fifth declension, long.

As also particles that come
In mode derivative therefrom.
Long second persons singular
Of second conjugation are,
And monosyllables in e.
Take, for example, mē, tē, sē,
Then, too, adverbial adjectives
Are long as rich old women's lives—
If from the second declination
Of adjectives they've derivation:
Pulchrē and doctē, are the kind
Of adverbs that I have in mind.
Fermē is long, and ferē also—
Benĕ, and malĕ, not at all so.
Lastly, each final *eta* Greek,
Is long on all days of the week—
To wit—(for thus we render nempe)
Lethē, Anchisē, cetē, Tempē.

Those words as long we classify
Which end, like *egotists*, in *i*,
Rememb'ring mihi, tibi, sibi
Are common, so are ubi, ibi;
Nisĭ is always short, and quasĭ's
Short also, so are certain cases
In i—Greek vocatives and datives
(At least if we may trust the natives;)
Making their genitives in os,
For instance—Phyllis, Phyllidos.
(A name oft utter'd with a sigh,)
Whereof the dative ends in ĭ.

Words in *l* ending short are all,
Save nīl for nihil, sāl, and sōl,
And some few Hebrew words t'were well
To cite; as Michaēl, Raphaēl.

Your n's are long, save forsităn
Ĭn, tamĕn, attamĕn, and ăn
Veruntamĕn and forsăn, which
Are short as any tailor's stitch;
These, therefore, we except, and then
Contractions "per apocopen"—
As vidĕn'? mĕn'? and audĭn?—so in
Exĭn' and subĭn', deĭn', proĭn'.
An, from a nominative in *a*
Ending a word is short, they say,
But every *an* for long must pass

Derived from nominative in as.
Nouns, too, in en are short whose finis
Doth in the genitive make *inis*.
And so are n's that do delight ĭn
An *i* and *y*—Alexĭn, Itўn.

Greek words are short I'd have you know,
That end in *on* with little *o*,
Common are terminating o's,
Cases oblique except from those,
Adverbial adjectives as falsō
Are long,—take tantō,—quantō also;
Save mutuo, sedulo, and crebro.
Common as vestment vending Hebrew.
Modŏ and quomodŏ among
Short o's we rank—nor to be long.
Nor citŏ, egŏ, duŏ; no nor
Ambŏ and Homŏ ever prone are;
But monosyllables in *o*,
Are counted long. Example—stō.
And omega, the whole world over,
'S as long as 'tis from here to Dover.

If *r* should chance a word to wind up,
'Tis short in general, make your mind up;
But fār, lār, nār, and vīr, and fūr
Pār, compār, impār, dispār, cūr,
As long must needs be cited here,
With words from Greek that end in er;
Though 'mong the Latins from this fate are
These two exempted—patĕr, matĕr;
Short in the final *er* we state 'em,
Namely, "auctoritate vatum."

Now, s, the Eton Grammar says,
Ends words in just as many ways
As there are vowels—five—as thus
In order, *as, es, is, os, us.*

As, in a general way appears
Long unto all but asses' ears,
But some Greek words take care to mark as
Short,—for example—Pallăs, Arcăs—
And nouns increasing plural sport
An *as* accusative that's short.

Es in the main's a long affair,
Anchisēs, such, and patrēs are,
Though of the third declension you

As short such substantives must view,
The genitives of which increase,
Derived from nominatives in es,
And have an accent short upon
The syllable that's last but one.
As milĕs, segĕs, divĕs, (which
Means what a Poet is n't,)—rich:
But pēs is long, with bipēs, tripēs,
Like to a hermit munching dry pease.
To these add Cerēs, Saturn's cub,
(Name of a goddess, and for grub
The figure Metonymy through,)
And ariēs, abiēs, pariēs, too.
Sum with its compounds forming ĕs,
Are short, join penĕs, if you please,   }
Item Cyclopĕs Naiadĕs.
Greek nominatives and plural neuters,
For lists of which consult your tutors.

Is, we call short, as Parĭs, tristĭs,
Save all such words as mensīs, istīs.
Plurals oblique that end in *is*,
Adding thereto for quibus quīs.
The *is* in Samnīs long by right is
Because its genitive's Samnītis,
Where you observe a lengthened state
Of syllable penultimate.
The same to all such words applies,
And īs contracted, meaning *eis*,
Long too,—and pray remember this
Are monosyllables in *is*.
Save ĭs the nominative pronoun,
And quĭs, and bĭs, which last is no noun.

When verbs by *is* concluded are,
In second person singular;
But in the plural *itis* make,
The *is* is long, and no mistake—
Provided always that the pe-
Nultimate plural long shall be.

Os, saving compŏs, impŏs, ŏs
Is long—as honōs dominōs.
The Greek omicron 's short, and that in
All conscience must be so in Latin.

Words should be short in *us*, unless
Authority has laid a stress
On the penultimate of any

Word that increases in the geni-
Tive case when us is long, the same
Pronunciation nouns may claim—
Declined like gradūs or like manūs
Though here exceptions still detain us.
The first case and the fifth are those
Singular; short as monkey's nose.
Long are mūs, crūs, and thūs and sūs
All monosyllables in ūs,
And Grecian nouns by diphthong *ous*,
Translated *us* by men of *nous*.

Lastly, all words in *u* are long,
And so we end our classic song.

And not our song only, but our work—the companion of our solitude—the object of our cares—for which alone we live, for which we consumed our midnight oil; and not only that, but also burnt a great deal of daylight.—Our work, we say, is ended—and such as it is we commit it to the world. Horace says Carm. Lib. iii, Ode XXX. (an ode which by some strange association of ideas, is always connected in our mind with the visionary image of a jug of ale,) "Exegi monumentum ære perennius," I have perfected a work more durable than brass. Whether our production is characterized by the *durability* of that metal or not, is a question which we leave to the decision of posterity; we cannot, however, help thinking that, considering the boldness of our attempt, it possesses figuratively at least, something in common with the substance in question—and we would fain hope that that something does not consist in *hardness*.

And now farewell to the reader—farewell, "a word that must be and hath been"—said a great many times when once would have been quite sufficient. We need not, therefore, repeat it; nor need we say how much we hope that we have amused, instructed him, and so forth; that being as much an understood thing to put at the end of a book, as "Love to papa, mamma, brothers and sisters," in a holiday letter.

Nothing, then, remains for us now to do, but to kick up our hat and cry

"ALL OVER."

FINIS.

Lector House believes that a society develops through a two-fold approach of continuous learning and adaptation, which is derived from the study of classic literary works spread across the historic timeline of literature records. Therefore, we aim at reviving, repairing and redeveloping all those inaccessible or damaged but historically as well as culturally important literature across subjects so that the future generations may have an opportunity to study and learn from past works to embark upon a journey of creating a better future.

This book is a result of an effort made by Lector House towards making a contribution to the preservation and repair of original ancient works which might hold historical significance to the approach of continuous learning across subjects.

HAPPY READING & LEARNING!

LECTOR HOUSE
LECTOR HOUSE LLP
E-MAIL: lectorpublishing@gmail.com